What Oth

Mickey Bonner has given
incredible gift. The lessons involved in this book, if put into practice, would change one's life and one's church for good and for God. I am so grateful to be able to commend it.

Adrian Rogers
Senior Pastor, Bellevue Baptist Church
Memphis, Tennessee

It is a pleasure to recommend "*KYMS*" Mickey Bonner's latest book to you. I have known Mickey and loved him and ministered with him for more years than I can remember. Mickey Bonner was a genuine man of God, and like you, I always wanted to know what he had to say. He says it so well in this book and it is something you will never ever forget. You will not only be impacted but also tremendously blessed by what you read.

Dr John R. Bisagno
Senior Pastor Ret., First Baptist Church
Houston, Texas

Alice and I had the privilege of working for Dr. Bonner twice: in the early 1970's as his crusade musicians, and in the early 1980's as his Executive Director. he epitomized the message of this book; a spiritual giant, our beloved mentor. The book you are holding is a manual for maturity. It will salvage your relationships and could even save your life! I strongly recommend it.

Eddie Smith, President
U.S. Prayer Center
Houston, Texas

I want to recommend that people not only read and ponder this book, but also get the duct tape out and keep their mouths shut.

Iris Blue
Iris and Duane Blue Ministries
Woodstock, Georgia

Do yourself a favor. No! Do everybody a favor, and read this book.

LeRoy "Skip" Smith, Ph.D.
Assistant Pastor/Spiritual Development, Sagemont Church
Houston, TX

MW01542736

"Not that which goeth into the mouth defileth a man: but that which cometh out of the mouth, this defileth a man." Matthew 15:11

Dear Reader...

It's the most destructive force in the universe! No, it is not a nuclear bomb, a chemical or a biological weapon: it is the tongue. Released without the control of the Holy Spirit, the tongue has the power to set our lives ablaze with the fires of hell ***(James 3:6)***. The only way to harness this devastating power is to KYMS! We are wise to follow Brother Mickey Bonner's profound advice, "Never speak until spoken through."

Most Christians don't realize how much the Word of God deals with the words of men. With our words we express the essence of what we are. In this book, Brother Bonner exhorts us from a heart broken by his own experiences and energized by the flow of the Holy Spirit. He reminds us that "we are what we say," and focuses our attention on this important problem which is rarely addressed even in the strongest Bible churches. If you have humility of heart, and the courage to face yourself as you really are, this book will transform your life. You will return to it over and over again as the Lord uses it to bring you to full brokenness and surrender to His will.

Pastor Duane Roach

"And if any one does not offend in speech - never says the wrong things - he is a fully developed character and a perfect man, able to control his whole body and to curb his entire nature." James 3:2b Amplified

God Told Me

KYMS

By
Dr. Mickey Bonner

Transformed Publications
Mickey Bonner Evangelistic Association
Houston, Texas

© 2003 by Mickey Bonner

All rights reserved under international copyright conventions. No part of this book may be reproduced in any form by any means, mechanical or electronic, including photocopying, recording, or by any information storage and retrieval system, without permission from the publisher.

All Scriptures used in this volume are from the King James Version unless otherwise designated.

Scripture quotations marked Amplified are taken from the Amplified Bible. Old Testament Copyright 1965, 1987, by the Zondervan Corporation. New Testament Copyright 1958, 1987, by the Lockman Foundation. Used by permission.

TM A TradeMark of the Mickey Bonner Evangelistic Association, Houston, Texas.

ISBN: 1-878578-18-9
Published by Mickey Bonner Evangelistic Association
PO Box 680368, Houston, Texas 77268-0368

Printed in the United States of America

Dedication

To the staff of this ministry in their tireless demonstration of their love of Jesus Christ. We are grateful to God for His workers in this vineyard.

I praise God for these who as our inner circle keep this ministry in decency and order by prayer and service.

This book is gratefully dedicated to these, God's choice servants.

Dr. Mickey Bonner

Contents

Appreciation To:

Pastor Duane Roach and LTC. Ted Shadid (US Army, Ret.), Mr. and Mrs. Matt Montgomery, and our Board of Directors- may God Bless you for your dedication to this ministry.

To all of those who have prayed and continually pray for this ministry. Thank You!

Devotedly,
MBII

Foreword

In this century we have seen God do some unusual things and one of these things has been the revival of certain doctrines of the Bible. I feel that the revival of these doctrines is because of having neglected them in some measure or another. For instance, we have had a strong emphasis on the doctrine of sanctification. As a result, we have gone through a revival of the doctrine of sanctification and related truth. If we are not careful, because of the neglect of this subject matter, and therefore, the lack of our understanding, we will be so cautious that we will not allow the Lord to speak to us at all.

This book, I believe, is a result of that revival.

Brother Bonner is one of the finest Christians I know. He has sought the Lord faithfully and studied his Bible prayerfully and I believe has come up with a neglected truth that relates to God, man, and Satan in a way that will bring Christians into practical Christian living.

My personal opinion is that we should realize that the truth of positive and negative confession is dealt with in the Bible. Therefore, we should face this study on the basis of what is truth about positive and negative confession and then believe that truth to the glory of God.

This book, *KYMS*, will take us through a very thorough search of the Scriptures and should leave us, if Spirit led, scripturally grounded.

Manley Beasley

KYMS

With Gratitude

Having the opportunity to read this book has triggered some exciting convictions and brought to mind some fond memories.

Within just a few days of my salvation, I contacted the Bonners and went to hear Bro. Mickey preach and to visit with them after the meeting. Coming from a background of drugs, perversion, prison and filthy talk etc., my life had already taken a great turn. My vocabulary had already been reduced to very few words, BUT hearing a message on Life and Death in the tongue caused me to want to duct tape my mouth. I saw how easy it is in trying to help people with warnings or example, to cause more bondage with my own mouth to the very ones I longed to help.

Now, 25 years later, having the powerful words of this book in my life again is a real blessing. I have read the book aloud to my husband, Duane, and son, Denim, while we traveled. At one point, we became so convicted that we pulled off the road to pray and seek cleansing from the harm and heartache we had caused in others and our own lives because of destructive talk. I praise the Lord for the message of this book. It has caused me to see Jesus clearer and me better, I want to read it over and over to help keep life in focus and to help me "Keep My Mouth Shut!"

Some of the things Jesus taught were hard sayings nevertheless, having a message in front of you to expose you to you is hard but ever so refreshing.

I want to recommend that people not only read and ponder this book, but also get the duct tape out and keep their mouths shut.
Thank you, for finishing Bro. Mickey's work.

With Much Love and respect,
Iris Blue
One of the many kids of Mickey Bonner in the ministry.

With Gratitude

Dear Fellow Laborers:

It has been my fantastic privilege to have just completed reading *"KYMS"* written by my good personal friend, the late Rev. Mickey Bonner. How exciting and electric it was to read over his words of wisdom and hear echoing again and again in my heart the powerful voice of this great Saint of God.

Mickey Bonner truly was "sold out" to the Lord Jesus. He wrote what he heard from the heart of God. He preached what he wrote and lived what he preached. From forty years of personal friendship with Mickey, I have observed the purity and genuine zeal for the Lordship of Jesus at whatever price required. Therefore reading "*KYMS*," was a reliving of that relationship as I read in words what I had witnessed in his life.

The unusual result to me from reading this book was to reinforce the Biblical Convictions the Holy Spirit has built into my life during fifty-five years of ministry. Not surprisingly it helped me establish *new* ones, ones I should have already had these many years.

It is with a sense of gratitude to the Lord for allowing me to have such a personal and brotherly relationship with Mickey that I can urge you to read this book. I personally went through several of the experiences spoken of in this book with Mickey as they happened. I therefore can validate their authenticity as well as agree totally with the biblical applications and scriptural admonitions given. The words of James tells us to ***"let every man be swift to hear, slow to speak, slow to wrath: for the wrath of man worketh not the righteousness of God" James 1:19-20***. The wisest man who ever lived puts it this way, ***" soft answer turneth away wrath: but grievous words stir up anger" (Proverbs 15:1).*** While the Bible encourages using soft words, wise indeed is the person who learns to bridle the tongue and at times, use "no" words at all. It is still true that ***"Where no wood is, there the fire goeth out," (Proverbs 26:20).*** So where there are *no* words: arguing and contentions will cease.

Do yourself a favor. No! Do everybody a favor, and read this book.

With gratitude to the Lord for the privilege of having prayed, preached, loved and suffered with Mickey Bonner in the wonderful service of Jesus.

LeRoy "Skip" Smith, Ph.D.
Assistant Pastor/Spiritual Development
Sagemont Church
Houston, TX

CHAPTER ONE

What You Say is What You Are

You can tell what a man is by what he says. You can judge a person's character by the words that come out of his mouth. To begin this study we must look at the Scriptural position on good and bad things that come from the inner being. In ***Matthew 12:34-37***, we find Jesus stating this position:

> ***O generation of vipers, how can ye, being evil, speak good things? For out of the abundance of the heart the mouth speaketh. A good man out of the good treasure of the heart bringeth forth good things: and an evil man out of the evil treasure bringeth forth evil things. But I say unto you, That every idle word that men shall speak, they shall give account thereof in the day of judgment. For by thy words thou shalt be justified, and by thy words thou shalt be condemned.***

Here Christ reveals the true test of an individual's relationship with God. The Bible shows this in many places. Christ declares that you will know the nature or character of an individual by the words he speaks. In ***verse 34*** above, He gives an example of people who are evil but speak good things.

Two-Faced

The Pharisees had witnessed the great miracles Christ had performed; yet they refused to accept His deity. Jesus pointed out that they spoke good things but did evil things. Then when they came face to face with that which was good, they spoke evil of it. Another translation describes Christ's response to this kind of character, as follows: ***"O generation of vipers, how can ye, being evil, speak good things? "***. He goes on to share that a man's heart determines his speech. Another way to say it is: *"You are what you say."*

In the King James Version, we find Christ's declaration: ***"For out of the abundance of the heart, the mouth speaketh."*** The heart is the personality of the individual. That is who and what you really are inside. The soul is the seat of your emotions as well as the source of the kind of character and nature that make up your person. Man is a trichotomy: body, soul and spirit. Body is the physical housing; soul is the personality and character of the individual; and the spirit is the dwelling place of God. So, that which is the "most" of the personality or the ***"abundance"*** is simply your real nature as an individual.

If you would like to know a person's true character, listen carefully to what comes out of his mouth. If one moment he is speaking things of God in joyous anticipation and the next moment is negative, critical, caustic or bitter about someone, the Scriptures make it clear this person does not walk with God in fullness; he has no revelation; he is not led by the Spirit. People who are critical of other people do not follow the Holy Spirit's leading in their lives. They cannot because their own speech separates them from God's revelation.

The true identity of a person is what comes out of his mouth. That is his real nature; his character; his personality. ***"For out of the abundance***

of the heart the mouth speaketh." The word ***abundance*** means "the greater part" or "that which exists in excess supply." In this case, if a person is good, he speaks what is good, and if a person is bad or negative, he speaks what is negative.

You can tell what a person is, in his relation to Christ or in his own character, by what comes out of his mouth. If an individual is critical, caustic, bitter, negative—constantly putting someone down, even him-self-you can know that person is separated from God's nature in his life. However, if he is constantly praising God for every good and bad thing in his life, never saying an unkind, critical, caustic, bitter or negative word about another person or circumstance, that person walks with Christ and has been "healed" in his own personality. This means unforgiveness and roots of bitterness are gone from his life.

Going on in this Scripture, the verse states: ***"A good man out of the good treasure of his heart, bringeth forth good things, and an evil man out of the evil treasure bringeth forth evil things."*** Christ declares we can discern good and evil by that which comes out of the heart of the individual through his spoken word. The heart is the soulish "knosis" or the person's real self. We will say this many times in this writing. You must understand that the true test of a Christian's walk with Christ is what comes out of his mouth. Good and evil do not have the same source.

The Bible teaches, ***"Sweet and bitter water will not come from the same well" (James 3:11).*** This means that if a person is sweet one moment, talking about the glories of God and the marvelous works of the Spirit, and the next moment is critical, caustic and/or bitter, one can know the status of that person's personality at that moment is evil. In order to speak good things, he has to cloud over the "water" by adding to it to make it sweet. However, sweet water from a bitter well is always counterfeit and untrue. We will go into this more deeply in a later chapter.

Gossip

In the ***36th verse*** of ***Matthew 12***, Christ states, ***"Every idle word that men shall speak they shall give account of it thereof in the day of judgment."*** To be specific, an ***"idle"*** word is any word that does not carry life or power. Let me state it another way: God allows us only two appropriate ways to talk about other individuals. We may only speak of them in prayer or in praise. If you see someone with problems in his life, you are not to take that individual's character and dissect it by a spoken word. If you do, it is an evident sign of a need in your own spiritual character.

That is not to say that if God, through you, wants to expose a sinful or harmful circumstance, that you are not to do it effectively. A man whom I trust greatly and under whose teachings I have sat for several years makes a profound statement concerning this matter. He clarifies "gossip" in its purest sense and form: "Gossip is when you are not a part of the problem or a part of the solution." In other words, if you are not a part of the circumstances that created the crisis, or if you are not a part of the solution, and you talk about it, you are gossiping.

Therefore, character assassination is a move of Satan to dominate the nature of man through the channel of conversation. That is, if Satan can get you to be negative about another person's character, direction, or circumstance, then he has assassinated in you the very nature and character of Christ.

You can know if you are living the abundant life and if you are truly operating in the spiritual realm. You can perceive this easily based on what naturally comes out of your mouth. God is specific in His Word. He commands us to pray for those who have problems in their lives. He also commands us to ***"pray for those who despitefully use us and perse-***

cute us" (Matthew 5:44). Later, we will show you that if someone says something negative about you, your response cannot be to take the issue and become defensive toward him by speaking negative words. God commands you to pray for that person. In fact, you have only two "rights" in the Word of God in this area. You have only the right to pray for him, or to praise God in what is being said.

Idle Words

The Scripture is adamant when it says, ***"Every idle word that men shall speak they shall give account thereof."*** Now, what is an idle word? Defining it again, an idle word is any word that does not carry life or power. For example, a person may be having a spiritual crisis in his life that causes him to move toward sin. This could include a myriad of things. God commands you not to verbally attack him or his circumstance but to pray for him. The person who is truly Spirit-filled and walking in Jesus will immediately move into a posture of intercessory prayer regarding the matter. He will not criticize; he will pray. He understands the origin of the conflict.

It is interesting to note that the Greek word used here for *"idle"* is *"argos."* It means inactive or unemployed. The implication is lazy, useless, barren, idle and slow. This is Christ's description of the critical person.

Herein lies a good test for you to see where you are in Christ. Do you create strife or crisis by verbally dissolving the character of an individual? Or, do you immediately go to prayer and seek the face of God on his behalf? I cannot be emphatic enough in this area. You must realize that, according to ***II Corinthians 5:10***, we, as Christians, are going to be judged for everything that happened in our lives after salvation. When we stand before God, the overwhelming sin most of us will face will be negative confession. God has kept a record of every idle word you have ever spoken. In a later chapter, I am going to show you that if you have even listened to gossip, you have given mental assent to character assassination. You will stand in as great a judgment as the person who did the speaking.

Literally, God intends for us to have nothing to do with negative confession. People who are soulishly sick assassinate other people's lifestyles. Do not be caught in that trap. Do not let Satan take your mouth and make it speak idle words that create crises in the lives of others. By doing so, you will eventually bring even deeper crises, not only in the spiritual as you stand before God in judgment, but also in your physical person here upon this earth. You can physically perpetrate crises by being negative. The Scriptures teach in ***Proverbs 17:22*** that a broken spirit dries up the bones. Here is the reason for a great deal of infirmities. When one constantly dwells on death, he partakes of its experience. The opposite of this is taught in the same Scripture. God says, ***"A merry heart doeth good like a medicine."***

Continuing on to ***verse 37*** of ***Matthew 12***, Christ says: ***"For by thy words shalt thou be justified and by thy words shalt thou be condemned."*** This is extraordinary doctrine. However, it is profoundly true, as we will see later from the Old Testament. You see, your words can completely devastate your walk with Christ here on earth. Very likely, the thing that hinders your "going on" with God is your negative confession. You probably wonder why every time you get started in the will of God and His "flow" through your life, something happens to destroy that experience. I believe you will find it to be your confession. The tongue is a power. It can set the course or break the course of human nature.

And the tongue is a fire, a world of iniquity: so is the tongue among our members, that it defileth the whole body, and setteth on fire the course of nature; and it is set on fire of hell. (James 3:6)

So, your words justify you. By the same rule, your words condemn you. Your speech either separates you from God through "idle words" or brings you closer to His will through praise.

Fool's Voices

Look with me at another area in the Bible that expresses this. I think one of the most profound statements I have ever read concerning the spoken word is found in ***Ecclesiastes 5:1-7:***

Keep thy foot when thou goest to the house of God, and be more ready to hear, than to give the sacrifice of fools: for they consider not that they do evil. Be not rash with thy mouth, and let not thine heart be hasty to utter any thing before God: for God is in heaven, and thou upon earth: therefore let thy words be few. For a dream cometh through the multitude of business; and a fool's voice is known by a multitude of words. When thou vowest a vow unto God, defer not to pay it; for he hath no pleasure in fools: pay that which thou hast vowed. Better is it that thou shouldest not vow, than that thou shouldest vow and not pay. Suffer not thy mouth to cause thy flesh to sin; neither say thou before the angel, that it was an error: wherefore should God be angry at thy voice, and destroy the work of thine hands? For in the multitude of dreams and many words there are also diverse vanities: but fear thou God.

As we stated at the outset, God has much to say about the spoken word. He begins this chapter in the Old Testament by declaring that we are to stay quiet when we go to the church.

I think one of the greatest tragedies in the Christian church today is what we call the "business meeting." God expects us to conduct His business in decency and in order. We are to conduct it according to the Word of God and under pastoral authority. You can find these principles in ***I Peter 5:1-5*** and ***Ephesians 4:11-14,*** as well as other areas of the Word of God. Satan today has the church so completely devastated and turned around that, in its confusion, it cannot hear from God. As a result, it does not know God's direction.

Why? Because of its procedures of business. The church is out of divine order. In fact, God specifically states in ***Ecclesiastes 5*** that we are to ***"Keep thy foot,"*** or focus on what we are doing and stay quiet when we go to the house of God. We are to go ***"and be ready to hear rather than give the sacrifice of fools, for they consider not that they do evil."*** God says that the person who is a fool considers not that he does evil.

Let me give you an illustration of this. How many of you who are faithful in the workings of the local church have ever known an individual who, during the course of every business meeting, has to have something to say regarding the business of the church? Inside you knew that this person was not an asset to the direction or dimension of God but actually a detriment. Now, I am not asking you to judge in these matters. Also, I am not encouraging you to be critical toward him. As we have stated earlier, you have only one position with a person like that—to pray for him or to praise God for him. You must never bring his name up critically to another person, for when you do, you separate yourself from God instantly. Nevertheless, looking again at the verse, we find God declares specifically people are to stay quiet and ***"Be more ready to hear than***

give the sacrifice of fools" in the house of God.

He continues in the second verse, stating, be ***"not rash with thy mouth, and let not thine heart be hasty to utter any thing before God."*** Then He emphasizes that our words are to be few. You see, ***James 3:2,*** teaches that the person who can control his mouth can control his whole life: ***"For in many things we offend all. If any man offend not in word, the same is a perfect man, and able also to bridle the whole body."***

God has a specific word for the person who talks all the time, for He says in the ***third verse*** of ***Ecclesiastes 5: "For a dream cometh through the multitude of business, and a fool's voice is known by a multitude of words."*** How can you tell a "fool"? He talks all the time. Then, in the process of his conversation, he never says anything worthwhile. People who constantly have a barrage of words demonstrate they live in a form of rejection. They are striving to be heard and to be accepted, thus the smoke screen of conversation. God says these people live in a dream world, and they are known for their much speaking.

Have you ever met an individual whom you felt you really needed to know and about whom you would like to know more? You were very excited about his personality—until that individual began to speak. Within the first few minutes you realized you had made a mistake. God says, *"Keep your mouth shut!"*

PROMISES, PROMISES

In going further in these verses, I must share the personal effect on my life of this next passage. God showed these two verses to me some years ago concerning His position on making a vow. God moved in my life and saved me in the Spring of 1953. I had come out of some tragic circumstances. I will not share these with you because God has forgiven and forgotten, so it is not necessary to go over them. However, when He saved me, I knew instantly that I was to preach the Word of God. All of my life I had felt that someday I would preach, even though my life was not involved in any way with Christ or the church or the Word of God itself.

I became a "born-again" Christian at the age of 23, which meant I had a great deal of mileage "in the world" before Christ became the central theme and figure of my heart. But when I said, "Yes," to salvation, it was not only to Christ's coming into my life and saving me. That "yes" was also a resounding and profound declaration of my life to preach the Word of God.

One month after being born again, I entered the military for a little less than two years. God began to develop my heart, but some areas of backsliding also came. The first excitement of that New Testament new birth had begun to burn out as I got around "older Christians." I found that I was not as excited as I had been. All they wanted to do was talk about "church." As a new believer, all I wanted to do was talk about Jesus. However, my priorities changed soon after I entered into a local church in Marysville, California.

After my release from service, I came back to Houston to begin college. My purpose was to study for the ministry. For the next three years, I began to move in another direction. I became music director of a local church. Eventually, my college major changed to business. Money became my goal, as well as my god. I changed to a larger church after a year and a half to become its music director. However, as Dr. R. G. Lee—a dear old saint and friend who is now with the Lord—used to say, "There will be a payday someday." And there was!

During the course of this moving away from God's perfect will for my life, God spoke to me very severely in the loss of three children.

Because I was His son, God was disciplining me through scourging to bring me back into His perfect will. You can find the biblical doctrine for this in ***Hebrews 12:5-8***:

> ***And ye have forgotten the exhortation which speaketh unto you as unto children, My son, despise not thou the chastening of the Lord, nor faint when thou art rebuked of him: For whom the Lord loveth he chasteneth, and scourgeth every son whom he receiveth. If ye endure chastening, God dealeth with you as with sons; for what son is he whom the father chasteneth not? But if ye be without chastisement, wereof all are partakers, then are ye bastards, and not sons. Furthermore we have had fathers of our flesh which corrected us, and we gave them reverence: shall we not much rather be in subjection unto the Father of spirits, and live? For they verily for a few days chastened us after their own pleasure; but he for our profit, that we might be partakers of his holiness. Now no chastening for the present seemeth to be joyous, but grievous: nevertheless afterward it yieldeth the peaceable fruit of righteousness unto them which are exercised thereby. Wherefore lift up the hands which hang down, and the feeble knees;***

During this period, He truly brought home to my heart the truth of the Hebrews passage on discipline and the Ecclesiastes passage on keeping vows. I had made a vow to God, and I had deferred to pay that vow. Or better said, I had made promises to God and backed away from them.

How God resolved this situation is indelibly etched in my memory. I was five years old in the Lord. Two of those years had been in the military service and three had been in serving the local church. In the meantime, I was also trying to build a subcontracting company, as well as attend school. I was devastated. My heart was broken. My home was not right. My attitude was not right. My life was separated from God, and the harder I "worked" at being a Christian, the worse things got. The reason was simple: I was running from God, and God always deals with His children as it pleases Him. So, under the pressure of the loss of the three children, as well as the conflicts in my business and in my own heart, I finally caved in and gave up my life to do God's will. Pastor friends were telling me that my ministry was singing. Others were sharing with me that God needs good businessmen. But God was saying to my heart: "You said yes to my call," and, in today's vernacular, "you'd better get with it." I was on my knees, broken before Him in prayer. At that moment, I gave my life back to God. I again said "Yes" to God's plan for my life.

As I ceased praying and felt the peace and release in my heart, I got up and walked from my bedroom into my kitchen. As I stood there for a moment, the phone rang. I remember vividly that as I turned to look at the phone, I did not know who it was, but I knew without a doubt what it was. On the other end of the line was a precious brother by the name of Ulysses S. Garrett, who had a one-room mission in a place, called San Felipe Courts in Houston. This was city housing for people who did not have the means to completely support themselves. I shall never forget what he said. His first words were: "Brother Mickey, we are going to have a revival at our mission. God impressed me that you are to preach the meeting. Are you a preacher?" I remember hearing myself say, "I am now." The results? We went into that little mission that had forty-seven members and, in five days, God gave us over fifty people who trusted Christ as their personal Savior and were born from above. The die was cast. The direction was established, and I began to confess that I was a preacher. God began to set the course of liberty for my life ***(Romans 11:29)***.

The Scripture adamantly teaches in ***Ecclesiastes 5:4-5: "When you vowest a vow, defer not to pay it; for God hath no pleasure in fools. Pay that which thou hast vowed."*** How many of you reading this have ever made a vow to God: "God, if you'll just do this for me, I'll do that for you"? How many of you have ever made a vow to tithe? How many of you have ever confessed the call to preach and have backed away from it? How many of you in your need have made a promise to God and you "deferred to pay it." God calls you a fool. You see, He says in the next verse: ***"Better it is that thou shouldest not vow than that thou shouldest vow and not pay."*** The point I am trying to get you to see is simply this: Your mouth can cause you such tremendous problems. Keep your speech clean; keep it clear; make no promises you will not keep. Never say anything that will cause conflict between you and God. This includes not saying anything that will cause conflicts in another person's life or nature. Your vow is your nature expressed. You are what you say.

Lost Rewards

Most people have no idea that their confession can separate them from God. I am going to engage in a little "Mickeyology" to make these points, if I may, please. Search the Scripture on this point and see if it does not verify the thrust of this teaching.

Let us begin with an illustration. Suppose as a Christian, you have been very faithful in service to the Lord. Through you, God has been able to perform many things. He has not only developed His character through your life, but has exposed His precious Son to other people through your testimony or witness, or just by the life you live. You see, the rewards you receive in Heaven are not for what you have done for God, but what God has been able to do through you based on your obedience to His will.

Let us say you are obedient in every way to Christ and His control of your person. You are walking in the Spirit, led of the Spirit, living in victory. There is much fruit evident in your life as spoken of in ***John 15*** and ***Galatians 5***. You stay attached to the Vine. Jesus promotes His will through your life. However, somewhere along the way, you lose control, and in conversation you begin to assassinate someone's character (even your own) or perhaps you criticize the direction that your church is going. Do you know what you have done at that point? You have reached into heaven by your negative conversation and eradicated some of the rewards that you had received on the basis of your obedience to God. It ***"destroys the work of thine hands."*** Look at these verses. See if this does not verify it. ***Ecclesiastes 5:6-7*** says:

> ***Suffer not thy mouth to cause thy flesh to sin; neither says thou before the angel, that it was an error: wherefore should God be angry at thy voice, and destroy the work of thine hands? For in the multitude of dreams and many words there are also diverse vanities: but fear thou God.***

What does that mean? It means just what it says: your mouth can cause your flesh to sin. The most powerful force that you have within you is your positive or negative confession. Praise completely defeats the devil, as we find in the ***149th Psalm***. Criticism defeats the Lord's will in your life. Also, it destroys you from within your soul.

Negative confession separates you from God's "flow" through your life. You are what you say, and ***"Sweet and bitter water will not come out of the same well."*** God knows about everything that comes out of your mouth. In fact, the Word says that He is going to judge even your ***"thoughts and intents."*** Your mouth causes your flesh to sin. Your confession destroys your walk with God.

If you will study ***Psalm 139:1-4***, you will see the principle involved. God knows everything about you. He knows the complete personality that you are. He knows who you are and what you are.

> ***O Lord, thou hast searched me, and known me. Thou knowest my downsitting and mine uprising, thou understandest my thought afar off. Thou compassesth my path and my lying down, and art acquainted with all my ways. For there is not a word in my tongue, but, lo, O Lord, thou knowest it altogether. (Psalm 139:1-4)***

There is not one thought in your mind or one word in your tongue that God does not know the content and intent. You may be asking, "What is your point?" Very simply put: your mouth causes your flesh to sin. As Jesus said, it is not what goes in the mouth that defiles you. It is what comes out.

Let me give you another illustration based on the verses we just shared with you out of the ***139th Psalm***, along with the sixth verse of ***Ecclesiastes 5***. How many of you have ever made a negative statement about someone and then later that person found out about it and came to you and said, "Did you really say this about me?" Having been caught in the conflict, your say to them, "Well, that wasn't actually what I meant. What I really meant was ...". You begin to lie out of the circumstances. Has this ever happened to you? One thing really happened, and you stated something else. You did your best to get out of it.

I stand more guilty than all of you regarding this matter. How many times in the earlier stages of my carnal Christian walk have I been "caught," only to devise through my own mental ability some form of release from that relationship of guilt. I would lie or bend the truth to get out of the situation. Have you ever been confronted by another in this kind of circumstance? Well, if this has ever happened to you, God knows the intent of your heart. Satan has snared you unless you have confessed it as sin ***(I John 1:9)***.

The Bible goes on to say:

> ***Suffer not thy mouth to cause thy flesh to sin; neither say thou before the angel that it was an error: Wherefore should God be angry at thy voice, and destroy the work of thine hands? (Ecclesiastes 5:6)***.

What does it mean? When as a Christian you stand before God and the "book" is opened you will be judged for the life you lived, ***(II Corinthians 5:10)***. You will then be confronted with the true circumstances of every moment of your born again life. When a situation is brought forth and you reacted in criticism, you find yourself saying to the angel, "Oh, that isn't what I really meant. What I meant was ...", God shall intervene at that point and perhaps say to you: "No, that is wrong. I know the true intent of your heart. You've been caught." In fact, God says: *"Why should I be angry at your voice?"*

Do you see the depth of this statement? God says your voice will destroy the work of your hands, or rather, your rewardable ministry will be wiped out one by one with each verbal assault you make. How tragic! To stand before God empty, desolate, without reward. Your only reward is that you are saved, but "So as by fire." Why? You say: "I've been faithful; I've served; I've lived; I've tithed; I've given of my life. Where is my reward?" Destroyed—by negative confession! Study this and see if God does not verify this position to you. You see, God says: ***"Why should I be angry at thy voice and destroy the work of thine hands?"*** Of course, the principle of the ***"work of thine hands"*** has to do with the labor of service, based on your flow-through relationship with the Spirit of God.

Fool's Voice

How desperately important it is for you to understand how much power your voice carries as far as life is concerned. As we will share later from the Scripture, the spoken word is a power for good or evil. In the original language, ***verse 6 of Ecclesiastes 5*** uses the word ***"priest"*** for messenger or angel. This means you say orally before a third party of spiritual position: "What I've said I did not mean, or it was misunderstood." But, again, God understands the intent of your heart. Scripture goes on to say in ***verse 7*** that through this barrage of words, or in this case "many words," there is ***"futility and worthlessness, (Amplified)."*** And then He establishes: ***"... and ruined in a flood of words, (Amplified)."*** How important it is for you to understand that you can make or break yourself based on your confession. God's Word emphasizes: ***"A fool's voice is known by a multitude of words."***

How can you best judge the character of a person? By what he says. The Scripture adamantly states: ***"For out of the abundance of the heart, the mouth speaketh."*** In ***Luke 19:22***, we find that: ***"... out of thine own mouth will I judge thee."*** God will judge you for what you say, for what comes out of your mouth is what defiles and destroys or blesses you.

Focus Questions

Beloved this medicine is sometimes not easy to swallow. When you feel convicted, pray and repent. Remember guilt and condemnation are not from our Father. Now fasten your seat belts, and get ready for the ride of your life. We pray it will lead you to full enjoyment of the Spirit-controlled life.

1. According to ***Matthew 12:34-37***, How can you determine the true nature of an individual?

2. What are the characteristics of a "two-faced" person? How would you define "gossip"? What are "idle words"?

3. After reading the section *"Fool's Voice,"* describe how you can recognize a fool.

4. Read ***Ecclesiastes 5:1-7*** and state in your own words what it tells us about how we are to conduct ourselves in the house of God?

5. What does God call a person who makes a vow (promise) and does not pay the vow? Why does God make such a harsh assessment?

6. The most powerful force that you have within you is your confession. In this regard, what does ***Ecclesiastes 5:6-7*** mean to you?

7. How does negative confession separate you from God's flow through your life?

8. What things or rewards can we lose as a result of our negative confession (See ***Revelation 3:11***).

9. What is the meaning of the word "to judge" in ***Luke 19:22*** and ***Matthew 7:1-2***? Is there a difference in the meaning in the two passages? (Consult a Greek Bible Dictionary if necessary.)

CHAPTER TWO

God Hates

Do you know that God has the capacity to hate? This is one doctrine that always astounds many people. However, the Scriptures declare it to be true. When you understand just what God hates, I trust it will bring you to the place of studying your own life and "discovering your confession."

We shall do much research on this teaching out of the book of ***Proverbs.*** In this rich "Testament" God is emphatic about our confession. Solomon, in his wisdom and spiritual revelation, must have been a man who had great conflicts in this area. He saw by God's inspiration that a man who is negative, caustic, critical or bitter and expresses it to other people is spiritually sick. In almost every chapter we find reference to positive or negative confession. However, for this study, we will begin in the ***sixth chapter of Proverbs.***

Here we find God has the capacity to hate. The writer begins his instruction in wisdom in the second verse by stating: ***"We are snared with the words of our mouth,"*** and we are ***"Taken with the words of our mouth."*** Another translation says: ***"Caught in the speech of your mouth."*** I believe this amplifies the power of the spoken word. Through God's own declaration, we see that people who are critical, caustic and bitter are caught by the discernment of others. We find at the same time they will also have to face judgment for their negative confession. According to the Bible, people who are critical are ***"caught,"*** and their captor is God. Also, when you understand this verse you will realize your words are power. We will study this further in ***James 3:6***, as well as in the classic ***Proverb*** that totally explains what happens to the people who are critical. Their words not only catch them physically, but also profoundly impact them spiritually. Their speaking brings life or death.

As we go further in the chapter, ***Proverbs 6:12*** states:

"A naughty person, a wicked man, walketh with a froward mouth." One translation uses the word ***"worthless"*** in place of naughty. In the original Hebrew text, God says a person who has a perverse mouth is ***"worthless."*** Not only is he worthless, but he is wicked. The root meaning of the word *"beliyaal"* used here reveals its essence. It comes from the word *"belial"* which refers to Satan, the prince of evil.

A person who is critical, caustic or bitter is so consumed by Satan in his soul that it can be said he or she is full of the devil. Such a person is a child of the wicked one, a child of the devil ***(Matthew 13:38, II Corinthians 6:15, Acts 13:10, II Thessalonians 2:3, I John 3:10)***. Just as Jesus said to His disciples in ***John 6:60: "This is a hard saying; who can hear it."*** Hard or not, it is true. People who are critical are worthless in the Kingdom of God. God does not speak to or through them.

Then, in ***verse 12,*** God continues to say that the critical individual is not only full of the devil, but he has a froward mouth. No, I did not misspell the word. The word ***"froward"*** means (from Webster's Dictionary) "obstinately self-willed in refusing to concur, conform, or submit." In other words, they know it all. God says a naughty person has ***"frowardness in his heart, he deviseth mischief continually" (verse 14)***. Another way to say it is: he is powerless in the Kingdom of God. He has no direction from the Spirit of God. The Christian must keep himself separated from those who are critical ***(II Corinthians 6:17).***

The individual who is bitter, caustic, and critical of other people has no spiritual discernment, no dimension or depth of "Truth." Jesus Christ is, by and because of his confession, not the Lord of his life. Again, he is ***"worthless"*** and ***"wicked."*** Christians who have perverse, contrary, wayward mouths do harm to the ministry of God, as well as to His kingdom. They have no answer to prayer; and the most tragic position of all is they have separated themselves from God's will in their hearts. How tragic the existence of the person who is critical! He has removed himself from any real friends except for those who are in as diseased a state within their souls as he is. Most tragic of all, he has lost his spiritual victory.

Quick as a Wink

The kind of character I just described is easy to recognize as we find in the next verses:

> ***He winks with his eyes, he speaks by shuffling or tapping with his feet, he makes signs (to mislead and deceive) and teaches with his fingers. Willful and contrary in his heart, he devises trouble, vexation and evil continually; he lets loose discord, and sows it. Therefore upon him shall the crushing weight of calamity come suddenly; suddenly shall he be broken and that without remedy." (Proverbs 6:13-15, Amplified)***

As you can see, outward physical actions express the character of this person. God says he ***"winks"*** and he speaks by a ***"shuffling or tapping with his feet."*** He cannot stand still. He makes signs as he speaks, according to the Bible, to mislead and deceive, or to emphasize the negative traits of the character he is assassinating. He ***"teaches with his fingers."***

God goes on to say in the ***14th verse*** that he is ***"willful and contrary in his heart, he devises trouble..."*** Now, that simply means he has removed himself from God's Will. A person who is critical and negative toward other people, even by innuendo, God says, is not only "willful," but is "contrary" to the Will of God for his life. These people so freely sow the seeds of discord that it is evident they are out of God's plan. He says that they ***"devise trouble,"*** as well as ***"vexation and evil continually."*** As they speak of one thing critically, they are constantly looking for something else.

Do you know of a person who can find bad in everything? Perhaps about him is beauty, but because of his own insecurity and inadequacy he assassinates the character of another person. That person, according to the Bible, is spiritually sick. The Scripture goes on to say, ***"He lets loose discord and sows it."*** He looks for the negative in everything.

God declares, ***"a whisperer separates chief friends."*** In the case of the person who is ***"worthless"*** in the kingdom of God, the Bible says he ***"lets loose discord and sows it."*** He is constantly trying to cause problems or create calamity. He is a part of Satan's kingdom and Satan's work, which is to divide ***(Matthew 12:26-27)***.

Heavy, Heavy Hangs Over Your Head

Now, look at God's judgment on this person. God says in ***Proverbs 6:15***, ***"Therefore, upon him shall the crushing weight of calamity come suddenly; suddenly shall he be broken and that without remedy."*** God says the person who is critical, caustic, or bitter can look forward to calamity, problems, tragedy, and conflict. Why? Because he has given place to the devil, according to God's revelation in the third chapter of James. In other words, Satan has taken over his life and expresses himself through his mouth.

I must urge you to take no spiritual instruction from a person who is critical of another individual. Such a person has no spiritual revelation and speaks of external things from hearsay. We will discuss with you later how to separate yourself from this person in a spiritual way or, better still, how to help him to come into a spiritual dimension and have inner healing. A person who is critical and constantly negative in his confession is terminally ill in his spirit. He drinks from a bitter well.

Now, let us look at the six things that God hates from ***Proverbs 6***. Again, most people are not aware that God has the capacity to hate, but He does. Although we must point out that He hates sin, not the sinner. These verses clearly establish that fact. As you study these Scriptures, you will discover all six basically have to do with negative confession. Let us see this in the Amplified Bible.

> ***These six things the Lord hates; indeed, seven are an abomination to Him: a proud look (the spirit that makes one overestimate himself and underestimate others), a lying tongue, and hands that shed innocent blood, a heart that manufactures wicked thoughts and plans, feet that are swift in running to evil, a false witness who breathes out lies (even under oath), and he who sows discord among his brethren. (Proverbs 6:16-19, Amplified)***

Now, as we can see in the Word, God emphasizes His hatred for ***"These six things,"*** and ***"Indeed, seven are an abomination to Him."***

Again, you must understand God hates the sin involved, not the sinner. God does not hate sinners; He hates the sin. Christ died for the sins of the world by dying for sinners. That is why, for the Christian, ***"When we confess our sins, He is faithful and just to forgive us and to cleanse***

us from all unrighteousness" (I John 1:9). Perhaps you have been involved in assassinating someone's character through criticism. The simple procedure now is for you to confess what you have done and seek God's forgiveness and His will and purpose in your life. In the process of forgiving you, God may intend for you to go to the individual about whom you have been negative and also seek his forgiveness. You must close every door to Satan's gaining control again. In this case, you must close your mouth since that has been his door to enter into your life ***(Matthew 15:18).***

Now, beginning in the 17th verse, God continues by stating He hates a ***"proud look (the spirit that makes one overestimate himself and underestimate others)..."*** Pride is a presence of mind that allows an outside dominant control; by that I mean, a satanic intervention into the life of the person. Remember, the reason Satan was cast out of Heaven was that position of pride. You find this fact recorded in ***Isaiah 14*** and ***Ezekiel 28***. Pride is the door that gives Satan access and control.

God says in ***Proverbs 8:13: "The fear of the Lord is to hate evil: pride and arrogancy, and the evil way, and the froward mouth, do I hate."*** So, one of the conflicts involved in the life of the Christian dominated by satanic intervention is pride, and that pride will bring a perverse mouth. Of course, ***Proverbs 6*** more clearly describes God's attitude toward these evil attitudes and influences. He hates them! The individual who overestimates himself separates himself from God's will for his life.

In ***Proverbs 16:5*** we find: ***"Everyone who is proud in heart is an abomination to the Lord."*** Again, we find in a Scripture we studied in the last chapter: ***"A fool's voice is known by a multitude of words."*** There lies the statement of pride, especially the position of pride that God hates. He hates the sin of being a "know-it-all."

The Devil Made Me Do It

The second fact we find in ***verse 17*** of ***Proverbs 6*** is that God hates a ***"lying tongue."*** Again, we see how Satan consumes the speech of a Christian and causes negative confessions to come from a heart separated from God. The Bible teaches that Satan is the father of lies. The individual who speaks untruths has given himself over to the devil. Satan likes to consume the confession, according to ***James 3***. He delights in causing the person to become critical, caustic and bitter, or even to lie.

In ***Psalms 120:2-3***, the Psalmist cries out to God:

> ***Deliver me, O Lord, from lying lips and from a deceitful tongue. What shall be given to you? Or what more shall be done to you, you deceitful tongue? (Amplified)***

Here he speaks as if the tongue is a separate entity, one with a mind of its own. There is no controlling it from within. In essence, this is true, as we will see later. God says the tongue is a fire, a world of iniquity. It must be mastered. Its spirit must be broken.

People who have a tendency to lie need "deliverance." This is a demonic intervention in their lives that has created within them a spirit that is totally foreign to God's personality. In fact, they have "given over to a familiar spirit" that causes them to be negative. This is what God hates. He realizes the chronic liar has an outside influence intervening in his life that is not God - in other words, the chronic liar is demonized.

Further on in ***Proverbs 6:17***, He states: ***"And hands that shed innocent blood."*** There are several ways you can look at this. However, when you consider it in the light of negative confession, I believe you will find He is dealing with talking about other people in a critical way.

God hates the sin of those shedding innocent blood. He hates the sin in their lives, though, again, He loves the sinner. The question is, are you guilty of being critical of others? If so, then you have dwelling in you the sin that God hates so adamantly.

Then in ***verse 18*** He goes on to say: ***"A heart that manufactures wicked thoughts and plans."*** Here again, God specifically describes the soulish personality of the individual. God has a hatred for the negative side of that person's life. The word ***"manufacture"*** means to take something from a beginning source and put it together until it has become a product, or by-product, of that same source. In this case, people who by innuendo begin to create crises in the lives of other people are to be pitied. They are totally separated from God and need prayer and help according to the Word. So, the person who manufactures wicked thoughts and plans through gossip is one who has sinned greatly.

The whole problem starts by Satan planting a negative thought in the mind of an individual. Some other individual picks up just a small critical word dropped here or there. Someone else then takes that critical word and eventually so increases it in volume by negative confession that it causes chaos. How tragic! Satan, the author of confusion, has again won the victory in his work to divide ***(Matthew 12:25-26).***

Gossip

There is a game played in party circles where each person whispers a phrase in the ear of the person next to him, until it goes all the way around the group. After having made its oral trip from person to person, the beginning statement is compared with the statement at the end. Nearly every time so much confusion penetrates the statement that the end bears no resemblance to the beginning. It was not the same. The name of the game is "Gossip."

We can also illustrate the damage caused by gossip by taking a basket full of feathers and throwing them into a hundred-mile-an-hour wind. You might just as well try to repair the damage scattered by your negative confession after Satan blows it about with his foul breath. Oh, how he loves to play that game. In fact, he invented it — "Gossip."

This is how Satan works. He takes the negative words spoken by one person and amplifies them in the character of another who is just as separated from God. Eventually he succeeds in blowing the situation completely out of proportion. I can look back in my own ministry when people misunderstood the direction of doctrine that I was teaching on spiritual warfare. Through this kind of accusation that Satan orchestrated, I eventually had a label tied to my name regarding this important doctrine. This very likely has happened in one form or another to every individual who is reading this.

I'm All Ears

As we continue to study this ***Proverb***, we find that God addresses ***"feet that are swift in running to evil..."*** Here He refers to those who enjoy feeding off the carrion of another person's conflict or mistake. We will speak more of this later.

In closing this verse, God specifically considers two additional issues of character. First, ***"a false witness who breathes out lies (even under oath)."*** This statement relates to the judicial experience of life. God's imperative is that a person be truthful in all things. The "so help me God" that has been used by witnesses for so many years in court procedures illustrates this truth from the Word of God. God makes very strong statements about using His Name in vain, as well as about using any kind of cursing. God reveals His hatred for the sin of the person who would tell a lie on the witness stand. It is accentuated if that person is under oath ***(Ecclesiastes 5:4-5)***.

Finally, God makes the statement that is so relevant for today. In the latter part of ***Proverbs 6:19***, He says: ***"And He that soweth discord among brethren."*** How real this verse is for these times in the local church. We have no right to speak about another person under any circumstance except through prayer or praise. Any position or action other than this is gossip. Remember, you gossip when you are not a part of the problem or of the solution. If you speak anything other than prayer or praise regarding a matter, then it has become gossip. Gossip, in the New Testament, is an ***"idle word."*** Remember what we shared in the first chapter, ***"every idle word that men shall speak, they shall give account of it in the day of judgment."*** You see, that idle word is being negative toward another person (especially if that person is part of the ***"brethren"***).

For a child of God to be critical of another child of God is tantamount to criticizing God. No matter how deep in sin that individual is, God through the Word has given you strict procedures to follow in order to bring restoration of that brother or sister back to the fold. Someone has well said, "The Christians are the only army that takes its wounded and kills them." This means that, if a Christian falls into sin, God's commandment is to pray for him and try to restore him. Man's inclination is to be critical of him, to put him under. Better said, "Kick him while he is down." God says He hates this. *K.Y.M.S.*

Take the Test

God does not give us the right to be critical of another person. Man is made in the image of God. As we stated earlier, when we criticize another person, it is my belief we are criticizing God. Sowing discord among the brethren is a spirit God completely detests. Yet, when you check the life of the carnal Christian as described in ***I Corinthians 3:3***, you will find in his life envy, division and strife. All of this is perpetrated and perpetuated by negative confession. How tragic the control of Satan over the life of the individual who is critical!

Again, we have only two ways we can talk about another person-in prayer or praise. This cannot be stated enough. All prayer is warfare. If an individual is at fault, our prayers will restore him. This is God's way of dealing with error in the Christian's life. Prayer will "restore" such a one.

The litmus or acid test of where you are with God is your confession. The individual who walks with God never says an unkind or critical thing about another person. In fact, he will always find good and speak a blessing. The person who is separated from God and does not walk in His will, not only is negative toward himself, but sows discord among the brethren. Can you pass the test? These six scriptural positions we have just covered can show you where you are. If you are guilty of even one of these in your life, then you are separated from God. Again, God states, ***"For out of the abundance of the heart the mouth speaketh."*** You are what you say.

Out of the Mouths of Saints

Continuing in ***Proverbs***, we find God's repeated emphasis on negative confession. We find one of the strongest Scriptures, rooted in God's Holiness in the life of the person, in ***Proverbs 15:4: "A gentle tongue (with its healing power) is a tree of life, but willful contrariness in it breaks down the spirit." (Amplified).***

Much is said regarding the tongue in this chapter of ***Proverbs***. We read one of the most amazing statements here in the first part of ***verse 4***. God, through the writer, states: ***"A gentle tongue with its healing power is a tree of life."*** We could write much about the "trees" in the Word of God. In a study of this subject we find a tree illustrates Godly strength in a life living in the Will of God. The first chapter of ***Psalms*** states that the "Righteous person is as a tree planted by the rivers of water that bringeth forth fruit in its season." God says a Christian who is "abiding" produces a life-flowing fruit. He goes on to say, ***"Whatsoever he doeth shall prosper."*** The person truly planted by God's river or flow is an individual who has a ***"gentle tongue."***

Isaiah 61:3 also emphasizes this. There the individual who operates in the Spirit and has God's anointing on and through his life will be called a ***"tree of righteousness."*** Then God qualifies this person's ministry. He continues in the third verse by saying: ***"The planting of the Lord that He might be glorified."*** Who is glorified? God is. Therefore, He is emphatic in speaking of an individual who has a gentle tongue. That person will have healing power flowing through his positive confession. In fact, God goes on to say that person is a ***"tree of Life."***

Fruit of the Vine

The Scriptures we just considered do not stand alone in their illustration of this spiritual position. I believe we find the strongest illustration in ***John 15:1-7***:

> ***I am the true vine, and my Father is the husbandman. Every branch in me that beareth not fruit he taketh away: and***

every branch that beareth fruit, he purgeth it, that it may bring forth more fruit. Now ye are clean through the word which I have spoken unto you. Abide in me, and I in you. As the branch cannot bear fruit of itself, except it abide in the vine; no more can ye, except ye abide in me. I am the vine, ye are the branches: He that abideth in me, and I in him, the same bringeth forth much fruit: for without me ye can do nothing. If a man abide not in me, he is cast forth as a branch, and is withered; and men gather them, and cast them into the fire, and they are burned. If ye abide in me, and my words abide in you, ye shall ask what ye will, and it shall be done unto you.

In these verses in ***John 15***, Jesus makes the statement that He is the Vine, and we are the branches. The Vine is the Life; the branch is the Flow of Life. The fruit is Christ being Himself through that branch, the "abiding" person. Such is the individual who has no negative confession. He speaks only when spoken through. He is abiding in Christ and Christ's life is flowing out of him through his words. God says of that individual that his gentle tongue will not only have healing power but is truly a "tree of life."

The key to all true Christianity is listening. Have you ever been in a conversation that was dominated by a single individual? There were those there who had much more to say regarding the subject, but they were overcome by the dominance of the ***"fool's voice"*** who was heard ***"for their much speaking" (Proverbs 10:19, Ecclesiastes 5:3)***. God speaks in a still small voice. We must be able to hear and understand His motive and direction. This is the truth of ***John 15:1-7***.

We are to abide in Christ. He is the vine; we are the branches. When we choose with our life to become one with His, He begins to flow His ministry and will through us. We attach ourselves to the vine, and He lives through our branch (life). He then begins to produce Himself (fruit). Our life becomes His. The primary evidence of this is our fruit-bearing in answered prayer. It is also evidenced through our words. What comes out of our mouth is the declaration of what or Who lives within. ***"Out of the abundance of the heart the mouth speaketh."*** You are what you say.

The Trap is Sprung

Isaiah 61:3 says He is the source and the ***"planting of the lord thereof."*** Then He speaks to the other side of man's motive. In the latter part of ***Proverbs 15:4***, the Lord says: ***"But willful contrariness in it breaks down the spirit."*** Let me again emphasize, not what goes in the mouth defiles a person, but what comes out. To be defiled means to be made unfit, unclean, impure, or destroyed. If a person's character is defiled, it means something tragic has happened to him. Such is the case in the instance of a person who has experienced the tragedy of rape, molestation, or even abortion.

How many times have I counseled those who in childhood were defiled in some way? Through these incidents, Satan planted into these people the bitter seeds of the demonic. In my experience, I have never worked with a child molester who had not been molested to begin with. The same is true of a homosexual. Somewhere in their life Satan had set up a liaison to trap that life into the place of this incredible soulish death. The same is true with pornography. The trap is sprung, and the unsuspecting soul is consumed with demonic, uncontrollable lust. This is the meaning of being defiled.

Incidentally, if any of the above has happened to you, please understand there is a way out. Nothing in this world can stand against the Power of the Blood of Jesus Christ. No matter how far you have ventured into the depths, God is always there. He will make a way of escape through His Son. Jesus Christ died for the sins of the world. In that wondrous event that changed human history, He covered your sins also. He destroyed the power of Satan at Calvary. You are free in Him if you will confess your sins and ask Him to come into your heart. He wants to free you now. Believe me, He can. Nothing can stand against the Power of the Blood of Jesus Christ!

What Happened?

As we look further into ***Proverbs 15:4*** we see the Bible teaches that people who are negative, caustic, and bitter or who speak with a tongue that is not gentle, ***"break down the Spirit (Amplified)"*** within them. Please understand how desperately important this is. You begin a walk with God. You experience operating in His Spirit. You have His flow through your life. Then suddenly you lose your victory. In your spiritual defeat you say, "What happened? What did I do?" Very likely it is not what you did, but what you said. Satan set up a scenario to which you reacted ***(Ephesians 6:11)***. Instead of acting to it in praise, you reacted to it in anger. At that moment you opened yourself up to demonic intervention.

Christians who have their lips under the Spirit's control are the most dangerous to Satan. He cannot overcome them. Negative or critical confession is the strongest tool of dominance he has in his kit. He must bring you down to the negative. Again, what happened? How did you lose your joy? The answer is very simple. Go back, and you will find some negative statement you spoke in reaction to a person or circumstance. Christians who are critical stop God's power and flow through their lives. How many times has an individual met God in a spiritual way and then lost that wonderful victory through the tragedy of his negativeness? Criticism removes you from God. It is vital that you understand this. You stop the Holy Spirit's work through you when you become negative. ***"A fool's voice is known by a multitude of words."***

Is That Really Me?

During my two-year military career, I happened into a job as a radio announcer for the special services. This was a part of God's Divine Plan for my life in that 15 years later we began a daily radio ministry. I felt after several weeks of shows that I was doing quite well as a disc jockey and newscaster. That is, until I recorded one of the broadcasts and played it back. I could not believe it. I asked the individual listening with me, "Do I sound like that?" He said, "Yes, that's you." I was shocked at the true sound of my voice. My statement to my friend was, "Is that really me?" I thought it was terrible.

The same thing happens to an individual when he meets God in a "filling way." He is "filled" by having made Him the absolute sovereign Lord of his life, as in ***Ephesians 5:18.*** As God takes control of his life, the first thing he realizes is that his confession is not of God.

Isaiah 6 records a marvelous example of this. There, Isaiah "saw God." Now, no man has ever seen God and lived. However, when the Lord allowed Isaiah to look into Heaven he saw God's presence, perhaps as Light, and in that Light he saw himself. The illumination caused him to see his real person. He abhorred what he was. He then cried out for forgiveness. At that moment his life "began." Look at his statement in the fifth verse. Isaiah says, ***"Woe is me, for I am undone."***

Now, in order to walk with God and be filled with the Spirit, you must first see yourself as God sees you. At that encounter, the very first thing you will be conscious of is your confession. Isaiah declared this in the next verse. Hear his statement: ***"I am a man of unclean lips, and I dwell in the midst of a people of unclean lips, for mine eyes have seen the King, the Lord of hosts!"*** God revealed two things to Isaiah about himself. First, that he spoke negative and critical things. Second, he listened to others who were doing the same. They were a people of unclean lips. When God brought conviction to him, He cleansed him of his greatest problem, his confession.

Have you ever been around someone who has just met God in fullness? You find about his life a holy quietness. There is calmness and peace. On the other hand, the individual who is critical separates himself from God's power. The person who walks in the Spirit has only gentle words flowing from his lips. He speaks in meekness, quietness and calmness.

When God got ready to use Isaiah, the Bible says in verse six that He allowed seraphim to come with a live coal in his hand and place it upon the mouth of Isaiah. His lips were at that moment cauterized. This procedure was used as a form of healing. If a person received a wound and was bleeding, a red-hot piece of iron was placed in the wound to stop the bleeding. The process seared the wound and closed it. It also cleaned the wound of all foreign elements. Thus did God do to Isaiah. He seared his lips as a prophet so He could bring through him the message of the coming Christ.

From that moment on, Isaiah was a spokesman for God. The purging was not upon his feet that He could guide him, or upon the top of his head that He could speak to him, but upon his lips. Is it not amazing that when a man truly sees himself, his desire at that moment is to serve

God? That is exactly what happened to Isaiah. When God said, ***"Whom shall I send and who will go for us?"*** Isaiah shouted in response from his heart, ***"Here am I, send me."*** In his declaration he was pleading, "... Please send me! Please! I beg you to use me God!"

Take notice from this that God never sends the critical person. He may go, but he bases his decision on direction from his own spirit rather than on God's design.

We find a situation spiritually identical to Isaiah's in the book of ***Job***. Job was a man of great righteousness. However, his righteousness was involved mostly with self, as he declared in the last chapter of the book. Job's experience is an Old Testament example of man's flesh serving God. In the first and second chapters, God shows us how He protects us from Satan according to His will. Here He begins to correct Job for his backsliding, and we find the classic position of ***Hebrews 12:5-8*** beginning to work. God's "messenger boy," the devil, brings the chastisement and scourging.

Satan, with permission from God, devastated Job's life in the first chapter through his goods and his family. He brought chastisement. In the second chapter, he devastated him physically. Again, you must understand the devil did this only with permission from God, and to the extent that God allowed. He brought scourging. Again, please know that Satan is God's messenger boy and can do no more to the Christian than God gives him permission to do. In the third chapter, you find Job making the statement: ***"The thing which I greatly feared is come upon me."*** Job knew that something was wrong in his life.

Then you travel through chapter after chapter and find Job declaring, on one hand, that it is God who had brought this indictment to him. Then, on the other hand, we find Job trying to convince his friends how godly and good he is. Finally, God gets tired of this exchange of words in which character assassination contends with self-justification.

In ***chapter 38***, God steps in and challenges Job with the question which, in essence, reads: *"Where were you when I made the world?"* In other words, "I don't remember your being around when I did all these things." Job's major problem was he knew about God but did not know Him in his spirit. In his youth, he had obeyed all he had been taught about God, and God had blessed him beyond proportion. Then something happened within Job. He began to take credit for the work of God. Pride entered in, and God had to deal with him. He was 70 years of age when the events of this book took place.

In ***chapter 40***, we find that God makes a declaration to Job designed to break his nature and his will. He says, ***"Shall he that contendeth with the Almighty instruct Him?"*** Job was in a contest with God. He was trying to be like God. Then He goes on in His declaration, asking essentially, "Are you going to instruct or tell Me what I am to do?" ***"He that reproveth God, let him answer it,"*** says the Lord. In the presence of God, Job suddenly saw himself as he really was. Listen to his answer to God: ***"Behold I am vile."***

Now, that does not sound like the Job of the previous chapters. What happened to him? Well, Job saw God, and then he saw himself. His statement from there was: ***"What shall I answer thee?"*** He had truly seen himself. In the process, the first thing he declared was: ***"I will lay mine hand upon my mouth."***

What happens when a man meets God? He sees himself as he really is. His first revelation is his negative confession, his criticism, his anger, his cursing, and the violence of his speech. But go a step further. Job continues: ***"Once have I spoken, but I will not answer; yea, twice; but I will proceed no further."*** That was the end of Job and the beginning of God in his life; he died to "self." You can find his life declared in ***chap-***

ter 42. In ***verse three***, he says: *"I have talked about things that I have never known; I have preached about a God I never knew; but I suddenly understand the wonder of it all."* Then he cries out, *"Hear me"* (my paraphrase).

As he speaks to God, he begs for the complete fullness of the Lord's Presence in his life. For his statement goes on to say, in verse five: ***"I have heard of thee by the hearing of the ear; but now mine eye seeth thee."*** What is he declaring with his mouth? Praises to God. Nothing negative, nothing caustic, nothing critical, nothing bitter—just "O God, fill me with thy person. I want everything you have for me; in fact, I demand it. I can't live without it" (my paraphrase). For you see, here again, when you see God, you see yourself. When you see yourself, there comes repentance, restitution, and then restoration. Someone has well said, those are the "three R's of righteousness."

Saved, But Separated

Negative confession can totally separate you from the flow of the Spirit of God in your life. Returning to ***Proverbs 15:4***, the latter part, God states:

> ***A wholesome tongue is a tree of life: but perverseness therein is a breach in the spirit.***
>
> The Amplified states: ***A gentle tongue [with its healing power] is a tree of life, but willful contrariness in it breaks down the spirit.***

Here God uses the word ***"contrariness."*** In Webster's definition of this, he says, "being so far apart as to be or to seem irreconcilable." This is the work of Satan. His kingdom is to divide. He does this in order to fulfill the rest of the verse: ***"it breaks down the spirit."*** You must understand we either walk in the Spirit (Holy Spirit controlled and led) or we walk in the flesh (Satan's world system).

As we stated earlier, ***"Bitterness dries up the bones."*** Many times, I have seen people who are negative about everything. They contend and argue about anything. They are never pleased, regardless of what is done. I have also noticed these people have a tendency to chronic illness. They constantly complain. I have even heard them say, "I feel bad today, but I expect to feel worse tomorrow."

It is as in the old story. Two women were talking about how bad they felt. As each one describes her pains to the other, they were in a one–up–manship situation. They each tried to top each other's health problems. Finally, when one expressed she thought she had a bad heart, the other one, not to be outdone, stated, "I have horrible shooting pains, and those that are not shooting are reloading." Oh well, so much for the soul killing the victory and ministry of the Holy Spirit.

Incidentally, you can couple this with a verse used at the beginning of this book: ***"For out of the abundance of the heart the mouth speaketh."*** You are what you say. You must understand, based on this truth, you should never take spiritual instruction from a person who criticizes someone else. He does not know God in fullness, nor does he hear from Him in revelation. If your Sunday School teacher is critical by nature, pray for him: he needs help. He is just sharing with you what he read or what someone else shared with him. There is no revelation from God. If you have a spiritual leader who is negative in his conversation, I urge you to go to God for that person. Again, take no spiritual instruction or seek no guidance or prayer from a person who criticizes someone else. He does not hear from God. We will explain this more fully as we go deeper into this doctrine.

You must understand the exceptions to this. If a person is a part of the problem, or a part of the solution, he/she can discuss the matter with others who are also involved. A second exception is a person whom the Lord uses to reveal sin to another individual. However, in doing so, he must ***"speak the truth in love" (Ephesians 4:15)***. When covered in grace, the thing said will bring life and not death.

In His Word, God says the person who is contrary with his tongue has broken down the spirit. He has separated himself from God. Are you guilty? Have you ever asked the question: "Why can't I hear from God?" Examine yourselves and your confession.

Focus Questions

1. According to ***Proverbs 6:12*** what are the characteristics of a man who has a "perverse" or "froward" mouth?

2. What are some outward physical manifestations of a critical person?

3. According to ***Proverbs 6:16-19*** what are the seven things the Lord hates? Does it surprise you that the Lord hates? *Remember: God hates the sin involved, not the sinner.*

4. The Bible teaches that Satan is the father of lies. The individual who speaks lies is given over to the devil. What do these people need?

**Pray to God asking Him to write this on your heart and to recall it to your mind when you have a temptation to say something negative or critical. This will be a very valuable weapon of warfare against negative confession.*

5. The acid test to determine where you are in you walk with God is your confession. What does your confession reveal to you about your walk with God?

6. How does ***Proverbs 15:4*** describe a gentle tongue? Do you have a gentle tongue?

7. What does it mean to be defiled? How does our confession defile us?

8. What are you to do when you lose victory in your spiritual walk? How do you reestablish the flow-through relationship with Christ?

9. Before Isaiah became a spokesman (prophet) for God, what part of his body was purged by God?

10. Why are we not to take spiritual instruction or seek guidance or prayer from a person who criticizes someone else?

11. What has God revealed to you about your confession to this point? How would you describe the impact your confession has on your life?

CHAPTER THREE

Death and Life

Let's continue the study by looking at ***Proverbs 15:1: "A soft answer turneth away wrath; but grievous words stir up anger."*** God teaches that a soft answer turns away wrath. How are you to handle conflict? Quietly. The individual who resorts to violence by a barrage of words is one who does not have complete control of his person. That individual is unable to present himself a living sacrifice to Christ, as commanded in ***Romans 12:1-2***. Therefore, he is not Spirit–controlled, nor does he walk in the Spirit. However, the person who can stand in the midst of tribulation quietly can constantly deal with the wrath involved. How many times in personal conflicts have I seen this verse of Scripture come to life? When you deal with Satan's wiles, you must realize his position is to get you to react rather than act. When you subdue your desire to retort in anger, you have begun to bring your body into control ***(James 3:2)***.

The latter part of the verse says, ***"But grievous words stir up anger."*** The quickest step to violence is negative confession. This is the position of criticism, or caustic bitterness, exposed by verbal declarations. It is an incredible thing to read of instances of anger flaring into violence. While recently in a meeting in California, we read in the newspaper that on several occasions there would be shoot-outs simply over an altercation on the freeway. How tragic for a life to be violently injured or terminated for a momentary loss of self-control.

Are you able to stand quietly in the midst of a crisis, even though you may be right and the other party wrong? Can you handle it in praise?

You must understand that one of the words for Satan used in the Bible is ***"accuser."*** If the devil can get you angry enough by accusation to express either your position or innocence through violent speaking, at that moment you have been shot down from your place in the "heavenlies." God teaches that ***"grievous words stir up anger."***

The best way to tell the level of Christ's control in your life is how you handle the conflicts at hand, based on positive or negative confession. You are only mature to the level of your praise in the midst of your conflict. In ***Galatians 5:22-23***, God speaks of the fruit of the Spirit. One of these is ***"long suffering."*** The Greek word means to bear long with the frailties, offenses and provocations of others. Another is ***"gentleness."*** Here the Greek term means to be gentle, soft spoken, even-tempered. Then, another fruit is ***"meekness."*** The Greek term here means to be gentle, kind, without feeling the spirit of revenge. Finally, ***"self-control or temperance,"*** is the place of containing one's physical or emotional being.

Proverbs 25:15 is a beautiful verse that goes along with this particular Scripture ***"By long forbearing and calmness of spirit a judge or ruler is persuaded, and soft speech breaks down the most bonelike resistance." Amplified***

This verse means that if you can handle your conflict without being consumed by it, you are maturing. The writer speaks of calmness of spirit. This is the level at which Christ consumes your personality. This is basically a judicial situation viewed in this verse, but its point is that soft speech breaks down even the hardest most stubborn resistance. You are what you say, or in this case, what you do not say.

In ***Proverbs 15:2 (Amplified)***, God emphasizes through the writer that ***"The tongue of the wise utters knowledge rightly, but the mouth of***

(self-confident) fools pours out folly." The verse is open and self-explanatory. Do you add to the difficulty of a circumstance when you talk about it? Do you try to complicate the situation by emphasizing the negative points in the matter? If you do, then God depicts that which comes forth from you as ***"folly,"*** or for want of a better word, "unreal." Not only that, but the word ***"folly"*** has a basic meaning of "foolishness", which we will deal with more fully from ***Ephesians 4*** in a later chapter. I think the point must be taken from the original Hebrew, as it is not quite explained in the King James Version. Here, the word is ***"self-confident."*** The word ***"self-confident"*** in this position refers to the person who is "overconfident" and will sometimes relate to foolish jesting. God condemns this.

"Death and life are in the power of the tongue" (Proverbs 18:21); with it we bless or curse. To realize our own level of life or death, we must listen to what we say based on Bible declarations. ***"For out of the abundance of the heart the mouth speaketh."***

Pretty is as Pretty Does

In ***Proverbs 15:28***, we find that God says the ***" heart of the righteous studieth to answer."*** In this case, there is no snap decision, no immediate spoken word. This person has learned the process of waiting on the Lord. He has truly learned not to speak until spoken through. He no longer speaks his mind, but instead waits for the mind of Christ. Continuing with the verse, God says: ***"the mouth of the wicked poureth out evil things."*** The wicked speak negative confession. I have noticed that people who walk deeply with God never criticize. Also, they never listen to criticism.

We discover another test of the dimension of your walk with God in this same chapter, ***verses 31-32:***

> ***The ear that heareth the reproof of life abideth among the wise. He that refuseth instruction despiseth his own soul: but he that heareth reproof getteth understanding, (KJV).***

> ***The ear that listens to the reproof that leads to or gives life will remain among the wise. He who refuses and ignores instruction and correction despises himself, but he who heeds reproof gets understanding (Proverbs 15, Amplified).***

Are you able to take reproof? How would you feel if someone came to you and said that you need to change a certain area of your life? Could you handle that? One of the hardest things for me to face in my life is for someone to share with me some negative aspects of my person or personality. How I feel and react exposes to me where I am in Christ at that moment. If I defend rather than listen, I am separated from God's will. How you handle correction shows the depth of your walk with God. If you refuse instruction or ignore it, God says you despise yourself. In fact, one of the keys to knowing if you have the problem of rejection in your life is finding out if you can handle reproof. An individual who cannot stand admonition is living from past insecurities and rejection.

As this verse states, the person who cannot handle another's correction of his life despises himself. If someone rightly corrects you, and you take offense to it, there is but one word defining the conflict: rejection. How lonely is its banishment from reality! It is a prison of darkness and loneliness. Its walls increase in height as a person in this place becomes more and more negative and critical. It continues to blot out the light of the sun (Son) and becomes a dungeon of despair. Rejection is the place of accusation from Satan that destroys your victory in Jesus.

WORTHLESS CHRISTIANS

Moving into the ***16th chapter*** of ***Proverbs***, God again establishes the evil of negative confession. In the ***27th verse***, we find the formula for a "worthless individual":

> ***An ungodly man diggeth up evil: and in his lips there is as a burning fire, (KJV).***

> ***A worthless man devises and digs up mischief, and in his lips there is as a scorching fire. (Proverbs 16:27, Amplified).***

God exposes him as being a person who devises and thinks up mischief. The word ***"devise"*** in this case means to study a situation and conclude a negative response, then originate some critical statement about it. In other words, the origin of gossip springs from that individual. After spoken, it spreads like a cancer till it brings death. In the King James Version of the Bible, the word ***"worthless"*** is translated "ungodly" or one separated from the control of God's Spirit. In this case, he looks for evil in everything.

Then God takes us one step further; He talks about a person who ***"digs up mischief"*** as being ***"worthless."*** God is talking about the individual who suspects that something might be wrong and then begins working to find out the incriminating details. After discovering the negative side, he spreads the gossip around. In most cases, he fabricates innuendoes into lies in order to make them seem more significant. By this means he ruins a person's character or testimony. Satan has made criticism an art form.

This fact was brought home to me recently in a situation where two preachers confronted each other publicly. It began when one heard what another said about him. Satan began his work. It went from accusation to accusation, finally culminating at a spiritual gathering. Needless to say, God's Spirit was quenched. The tragedy of this event was that it all began with a word of gossip. From there, someone implied sexual impurity. It finally ended in a separation between ministers and the community, based on whose friend was whose. How tragic. It all began with a "so-called" meaningful friend expressing what he had heard about another. Demoniacal accusation! ***(Matthew 12:26).***

I cannot emphasize more strongly to the reader that, according to the Word of God, people who spread gossip are sick in their souls. I urge those who have revelation in this teaching to separate yourselves from a person who is bound by criticism ***(II Corinthians 6:14).*** In a moment, we are going to share with you that people who do not do so give mental assent to the sin. God commands you, ***"Be ye separate."***

Spiritual Perverts

Looking at the ***28th verse*** of this chapter, we find God making an even stiffer judgment: ***"A perverse man sows strife, and a whisperer separates close friends." (Proverbs 16:28, Amplified)***

He states here that a person who is critical of another person, or who ***"sows strife,"*** is perverse. The dictionary defines a person who is perverse as one deviating from "what is considered right or acceptable." Other definitions are "wicked," as well as "persisting in error or fault." The root word for "perverse" is the word "pervert." The dictionary's explanation for "pervert" is "to cause to turn from what is considered right, natural, or true; misdirect; lead astray; corrupt." For the most part, we think of a pervert as one who commits only sexual perversions. However, in this case, God says the individual who turns truth into error by simply blowing it out of proportion is ***"perverse".***

Look at God's feelings about the one who spreads gossip. He says ***"A perverse man sows strife."*** Please remember the origin of this statement is God. For a person to be caustic, critical, negative, bitter, or unkind in his statements is for him to say: "I deny God's control over my life." However, a person who controls his speech is able to give himself to God fully. How much stronger can God get regarding negative confession? There is no room for it in the life of a Christian. When a Christian manifests negative confession, it is a sign of his separation not only from the Spirit of God, but from the walk of God in his life. His confession controls him rather than he controlling it. This is Satan's playground. He sets the rules and wins every game.

Psst, Have You Heard?

The Lord further states in this verse that a ***"Whisperer separates close friends."*** How many of you have ever gotten around someone to whom you were very close and noticed he acted a little strangely? You could not understand his attitude. Later you found out that he had "heard something regarding your relationship." This magnified conflict in his heart and caused separation. God is very demanding in His statements toward gossip and sews them together with ***Proverbs 16:28***. It is tantamount to perversity when an individual talks about another person in a critical way in order to try to separate their friendship. This is an evident sign of sickness of the soul.

You say, “Ah, well, that leaves me out – I never criticize anyone; I’m never negative about a thing; therefore, I must be pure in heart.” Let me ask you this: Do you listen to gossip? Do you listen to negative confession regarding relationships of others or their circumstances? What do we mean by “circumstances” in this case?

Consider this example: A “church-fight” would never get started if no one fed the flame by negative confession. If there seemed to be a crisis developing, godly Christian people who walk in the depth of God’s will for their lives would never speak a critical word. In fact, these people would find a place to pray and enter into warfare against Satan. They would realize the problem was from him. “But,” you say, “I don’t see anything wrong with listening if I don’t pass it on.” When you listen to gossip, you give mental assent to the problem; or better said, you “Give place to the devil” ***(Ephesians 4:27)***. Never forget that God says: ***“Rebellion is as the sin of witchcraft” (I Samuel 15:23)*** and one of the words for witchcraft is “whispering.” The Scripture emphasizes that the Christ-led person will not listen to negative confession.

Let me share this with you in ***Proverbs 17:4:***

> ***A wicked doer giveth heed to false lips; and a liar giveth ear to a naughty tongue, (KJV).***

> ***An evildoer gives heed to wicked lips, and a liar listens to a mischievous tongue, (Amplified).***

“Heed” means to give serious mental assent to or listen to. Also, I think we need to clarify the word ***“evildoer.”*** Some, would narrowly define the word to mean a thief, liar, or even a murderer. Perhaps the best explanation for it, however, is found in the root of the word, which arises from the position of "evil." The word "evil" means morally bad or wrong–wicked–as well as depraved. Let us go to the dictionary for the full explanation of this word: "Causing pain or trouble, harmful, injurious, threatening, or bringing misfortune." Therein lies the root meaning of "evil." Now, an ***"evildoer"*** is a person who practices these things. "But," you say, "I don't mean to listen." Yet, when you understand the principle of the verse, you will see that an ***"evildoer"*** gives heed to wicked lips–he listens to gossip.

Though you may not be out in the world conducting yourself at a level of evil, you still have the seeds for evil inside if you listen to criticism. Please look at this from God's point of view. Man was conceived in sin and, effectively, he lives in sin. This world is filled with sin. We are sinners, unrighteous, ungodly, filthy, and God must change us. As Christians, He accomplishes this by our daily agreeing with God for our lives ***(Ephesians 2:10)***, by crucifixion ***(Galatians 2:20)***, and by a daily filling of the Holy Spirit ***(Ephesians 5:18)***. In essence, when we are filled with His Spirit, we experience the reality of what we already are positionally at salvation in Christ, we become the righteousness of God. This produces the victorious life as found in ***Romans 12:1-2***, as well as ***Galatians 5:22-24***.

Death of the Soul

On the other hand, we have dwelling within us the capacity for evil. This is called "flesh." You can test your relationship with God and whether you are walking in His Spirit or in your flesh by how you respond to gossip when you hear it. If you refuse and reject it, then there is the evidence of spiritual maturity. However, if you give mental assent to and listen to these cancerous conflicts that plant their seeds of death in your own soul, then it is evident that you are carnal by nature. You are, by God's standards, an ***"evildoer."***

Then, God goes even further in that verse. He states: ***"And a liar listens to a mischievous tongue," (Proverbs 17:4 Amp.).*** Now, what does that mean? The Christian who listens to criticism, God says, has dwelling within him a "spirit of lying." Look at this example. You live before the church what you feel is the Christian life. You serve, you give, you fellowship, you are involved. In fact, by all respects you have an outward spiritual walk with Christ. However, inside you have one tiny flaw: you listen to criticism. God says you have the "spirit of lying" in your heart. You are lying with your life; you are not being what God intended. You are not free.

"But," you say, "I don't want to hurt anyone's feelings. If they come to me with conflicts about another person's life or circumstance, I do not feel it's right to just say to that individual, 'Let's pray for them.'" Why would you feel that way? If someone came to you and pointed a gun at you and was ready to pull the trigger, would you not say: "Please don't shoot"? I personally have experienced in my own life the way listening to negative criticism destroys the soul's victory and its walk and control by Christ. When another person begins to spread gossip and evil before you and speak it to your heart, it is the same as if he pulled the trigger by the first word he spoke.

You see, people who are critical of other people are sick in their souls. However, when you have received their violence by mental assent and have agreed by listening, their disease has spread into your spiritual life. "But," you argue again, "I cannot afford to hurt the feelings of these people."

Let me give you an illustration: How many of you have a friend who, every time you get around him, or speak to him, he comes out with something negative? Let's say that when you awakened this morning, you committed your life to Christ. You did what He commanded you to do, and that is, you turned everything you are over to Him ***(Joshua 24:14)***. You sought first His kingdom for your life, and his righteousness, which means "right standing with God." In your obedience, God begins to add to you His will for that day. (You will find the principle of this taught in ***Job 7:17-18***. God has a plan and purpose for your life every day, and when you meet Him and agree with Him, that plan begins to be functional in your life.) You have chosen Christ's path from ***Ephesians 2:10***.

Now, Satan sees that you are walking in the "light." You are to him the most dangerous type of person. Why? Because, for that day, not only are you able to communicate with God in agreement for your life, but God is able to "flow His will" through you. In the process of it, the world in seeing you, will turn its face to God and say, "I believe Christ is real. I have witnessed your life and walk with God, and I believe."

How beautiful to live in that relationship! Satan begins to wonder how he can institute ***"wiles"*** to stop this victory that you have ***(Ephesians 6:11)***. He begins to coordinate the path of your best friend. He sees you working on your grocery list and plants seeds in the mind of this friend to go shopping. Eventually, through coordination, you find yourself at the same store - you have not run into each other yet; that is being carefully worked out by demonic forces. Finally, you meet - guess where - the checkout line. Two people are in front of you, your best friend behind you, and behind this person are two more people with loaded carts, waiting patiently for their turns at the register. You begin small talk, based on your friendship. Suddenly, your best friend has interjected from the sin–diseased area of his mind the thought to share with you something he heard. If you are walking with God and in His Spirit, as he begins to speak a guarded feeling will immediately come inside in your spirit-man, sensing the venom pouring out of his wounded spirit as he accentuates the negatives. You suddenly become aware that you are trapped.

You ask, "What can I do?" Very simple. If you walk with God, unashamed and unafraid, you will immediately stop that individual and say, "Let's pray for that person." Do you mean to say stop in that checkout line and pray for him? Absolutely. Why? Realize that person is "living in the dirt of his spiritual experience" and you are "soaring in the heavenlies as an eagle." If you can get that individual to pray for the person they are criticizing or talking about, you are going to bring them up to your level of spiritual walk.

You say, "Suppose when we finish praying for that person they are talking about they continue?" Then you simply stop and say, "Well, let's pray again." Eventually, they will get the message. At this point, one of two things will happen. You will either bring your friend to the level of your walk with Christ, or, if he is bound by satanic carnal dominance in his heart, he is going to think you are some kind of "spiritual nut" and leave you alone. May I share with you, that will be the greatest single circumstance that could happen to you in your relationship with that individual. Otherwise, he will continue to tear down your walk with Christ.

God hates gossip! He tells us time and again in this marvelous book of ***Proverbs*** about the tongue itself. ***Proverbs 17:27 states:***

> ***He that hath knowledge spareth his words: and a man of understanding is of an excellent spirit, (KJV).***

> ***He who has knowledge spares his words, and a man of understanding has a cool spirit, (Amplified).***

He teaches that a man of knowledge is a quiet person. He describes him with a term our young people have used for a number of years in speaking of someone who "has it all together." In teenage jargon, this person is "cool." God says a person who spares his words is a man not only of understanding, but he also has a "cool spirit." In this case, he has gotten it together, sharp, on top of it all. I love Webster's definition here. He states, "freed or giving the impression of freedom from all agitation or excitement."

Truth or Consequences

We find more truth in this area in ***Proverbs 18:20-21:***

> ***A man's belly shall be satisfied with the fruit of his mouth; and with the increase of his lips shall he be filled. Death and life are in the power of the tongue: and they that love it shall eat the fruit thereof, (KJV).***

> ***A man's moral self shall be filled with the fruit of his mouth, and with the consequence of his words he must be satisfied (whether good or evil). Death and life are in the power of the tongue, and they who indulge it shall eat the fruit of it (for death or life). (Amplified)***

In ***verse 20***, we find that a man's confession reveals his morality. If he speaks critical or perverted things, this shows his moral condition. If his tongue is perverted or slanted to the negative, you know the ***"abundance of his heart"*** is negative. However, the one who speaks only good constantly, is never unkind or critical, and cannot stand to be around criticism, demonstrates good character and a healthy moral self.

But the overwhelming power of ***verse 20*** is that a man must stand in the consequence of what he says. What does it mean? It means that what comes out of his mouth by spoken word demonstrates the power controlling his life for good or evil. The person who can control his lips can control his whole body. If a man speaks evil, he is evil. If a person is critical, caustic or bitter, he is soulishly sick. This could eventually even bring him to physical illness. We have already covered this in this writing.

Death and Life in the Tongue

In the ***21st verse*** we find one of the most important statements regarding confession. God says, ***"Death and life are in the power of the tongue and they that love it shall eat the fruit thereof."*** This reminds me of something a friend told me a number of years ago. I know this man, and I know the other people involved. I saw the miracle.

His mother was going into the hospital for some major surgery. He knew the principle of this verse and the power of positive and negative confession. On the Sunday before her surgery on Monday, he went before her Sunday School class and said the following to those precious elderly ladies:

"My mother is going in for surgery in the morning. She has been your Sunday School teacher for years. I am going to ask you to do one thing for us, and that is not to make one negative statement about her condition. I realize that this is radical surgery and that there could be a conflict involved. However, I urge you to speak nothing but positive statements: to confess only that she is going to get well. To declare that her recovery will be quick and that the surgery will do the work that must be done."

These precious ladies agreed and began to make a prayerful "positive confession."

The mother entered into extensive surgery on Monday, expecting to be an invalid for a number of weeks. However, two days later, she was up walking. Five days later she was eating solid foods and in such physical shape that the doctor said she could go home. The convalescence, he said, was expected to last for several weeks before any real normal signs of strength would return. However, within a week's time this woman was able to have some partial recovery and in two weeks returned to her son's business to answer the phone and act as receptionist. The doctor called it a miracle, and it was! However, the miracle involved was the miracle of positive confession. Our words are power.

We can use words to bind another person's life by speaking negatively about him. Or we can loose his life by speaking positively about him. In essence, confession is a form of praying. Negative words give Satan power. Positive words bring God's glory into the matter. This book cannot contain enough pages to record all the miracles we have seen when Christians broke strongholds on the basis of praise. By that I mean these Christians made positive confessions about negative experiences in the lives of other people. As we stand in the course of a conflict on the basis of praise, we defeat Satan. This is done with simplicity when we do it in the power of God ***(Psalm 149:6)***.

Yes, death and life are in the power of the tongue. If we only knew how much power we have, based on confession, then the verse in ***James 3:6*** would suddenly come alive to us. It states:

> ***And the tongue is a fire, a world of iniquity; so is the tongue among our members, that it defileth the whole body; and setteth on fire the course of nature; and it is set on fire of hell.***

I have a pastor friend who felt that this teaching was reading more into ***Proverbs 18:20*** than it contained. His statement was that there was no such thing as a "spoken curse." However, God always moves a person into experience to teach His point. Circumstances brought a great deal of negative confession toward this friend - so much so that the pressure became critical in his life and ministry. As he sought God in the needed areas, the Holy Spirit led him to confront Satan by declaring that all negative words spoken against him and his family be broken. They were. He later told me that since doing this, he had never been as free in his life.

It works! Also, as a person prays, he must declare that every word he has spoken negatively regarding himself or someone or something else be broken also. Again, in the Amplified version of ***Proverbs 18:21, "death and life are in the power of the tongue, and they who indulge it shall eat the fruit of it for death or life."***

We have dealt with the first part of this verse. Now, we must see by God's own statement the results of our confession. If we speak death (critical, caustic, bitter), we will live death. In this case Satan binds us in depression or rejection. We always live under the circumstances of the moment. If we speak life, we will live or give life in its abundance ***(John 10:10)***. This is God's statement. Our confession rules our lives. God states: ***"Those who indulge it shall eat the fruit of it [for death or life]."*** You are what you say. This is profound doctrine, but by God's own words, it must be adhered to. Satan is alive and well and as God says in ***I Peter 5:8-9:***

> ***Be sober, be vigilant; because your adversary the devil, as a roaring lion, walketh about, seeking whom he may devour.***

Death and Life

Whom resist steadfast in the faith, knowing that the same afflictions are accomplished in your brethren that are in the world.

Control your lips and you can control your whole body.

I urge you to begin to make a positive confession. I urge you to stand in the midst of your conflicts and praise the Lord for them. This breaks every bond and hold that Satan has in your life. I urge you to thank God in everything that is wrong ***(James 1:2-4)***. It is your words that express your true inner person. ***"For out of the abundance of the heart, the mouth speaketh."*** If you never speak a critical, caustic, unkind bitter word about another person, it is evident that there is maturity in your life. You demonstrate your maturity when you have a quiet, meek spirit and you never loose a barrage of negative speaking regarding circumstances.

Proverbs says many other things about the subject of confession. However, I believe God's wisdom on this matter is best expressed in the declaration that ***"Death and life are in the power of the tongue."*** What do you speak, death or life? You are what you say!

Focus Questions

1. Are you able to stand in the midst of a crisis involving conflict even though you may be right and the other party wrong, and handle it in praise? If not, why do you think you are unable to do this? The best way to tell the level of Christ's control in your life is how you handle conflicts.

2. The way you handle correction is another indicator of the depth of your walk with God. What two things are behind a person's not

being able to receive reproof? Are you able to receive reproof or correction?

3. In ***Proverbs 16:28*** what is the meaning of the word perverse? Have you ever experienced a perverse man or woman in the sense of this verse? What effect did they have on you and others?

4. In your own experience, what are some characteristics of critical people?

5. What should godly Christians do when a crisis develops in the church?

6. What does it mean that a man must stand in the consequence of what he says?

7. As Christians words are spoken about us, what should we do?

8. ***"Death and life are in the power of the tongue."*** Your words express the "power of the tongue." Your words express your true inner person, ***"for out of the abundance of the heart the mouth speaketh."*** Do you have a positive confession? Do you stand in the midst of your conflicts and praise the Lord? Do you thank God in every circumstance even when things seem to be going wrong? What do you speak, life or death?

9. Spend some time in prayer asking the Lord to reveal to you areas of negative confession in your own life.

Death and Life

CHAPTER FOUR

God is Grieved

Strip yourselves of your former nature—put off and discard your old unrenewed self—which characterized your previous manner of life and becomes corrupt through lusts and desires that spring from delusion; And be constantly renewed in the spirit of your mind—having a fresh mental and spiritual attitude; And put on the new nature (the regenerate self) created in God's image, (Godlike) in true righteousness and holiness. Therefore, rejecting all falsity and done now with it, let everyone express the truth with his neighbor, for we are all parts of one body and members one of another. When angry, do not sin; do not ever let your wrath—your exasperation, your fury or indignation—last until the sun goes down. Leave no (such) room or foothold for the devil—give no opportunity to him. Let the thief steal no more, but rather let him be industrious, making an honest living with his own hands, so that he may be able to give to those in need. Let no foul or polluting language, nor evil word, nor unwholesome or worthless talk (ever) come out of your mouth; but only such (speech) as is good and beneficial to the spiritual progress of others, as is fitting to the need and the occasion, that it may be a blessing and give grace (God's favor) to those who hear it. And do not grieve the Holy Spirit of God, (do not offend, or vex, or sadden

Him) by Whom you were sealed (marked, branded as God's own, secured) for the day of redemption—of final deliverance through Christ from evil and the consequences of sin. Let all bitterness and indignation and wrath (passion, rage, bad temper) and resentment (anger, animosity) and quarreling (brawling, clamor, contention) and slander (evil-speaking, abusive or blasphemous language) be banished from you, with all malice (spite, ill will or baseness of any kind). And become useful and helpful and kind to one another, tenderhearted (compassionate, understanding, loving hearted), forgiving one another (readily and freely), as God in Christ forgave you." (Ephesians 4:22-32, Amplified)

In his writing to the Church at Ephesus, Paul dealt very severely with the area of negative confession. He began by encouraging the Christians to be constantly filled with Christ. He said over and over in the book of Ephesians that they were to be "in Christ." He declared they were to walk in the realm of the will of God for their lives. He admonished them to find the paths God laid out for them and to operate in the heavenly places in Christ Jesus.

He spoke of a mystery in the third chapter. That mystery was Christ in their lives. He declared that they would be ***"fellow heirs and of the same body and partakers of the promise in Christ by the Gospel," (Ephesians 3:6).*** He spoke of their being granted the riches of the Glory of God that they ***"might be strengthened with the might of His Spirit in the inner man," (Ephesians 3:16).*** He continued to show them how the Lord constructed His church. He showed them how the ministry of the body operates and how God-called ministers to the body operate on the basis of their gifts ***(Ephesians 4:21).*** From there he moved into a warning position.

Beginning in ***Ephesians 4:22***, he admonished them to put off the former conversation (conduct, behavior, manner of life) of the "old man." The old man has the spirit and nature of the devil ***(II Corinthians 5:17)***. He describes that nature as ***"corrupt according to the deceitful lusts."*** Paul desired that they would put off and discard the old nature and walk in the fullness of Christ's fellowship and ministry through their lives. In the ***23rd verse*** he urged them to be renewed in the Spirit of their minds. That simply means he desired them to walk daily in the Will of God and in the Mind of God according to the revelation of God. You find the same position when Paul admonished the church in Rome ***(Romans 12:1-2)***.

He continued by asking them to put on the new man by an active reckoning on their part. The believer clothes the old man with the new man as the old man dies through constant crucifixion. He served us notice of this in ***Galatians 2:20*** when he proclaimed we are already crucified in Christ at the moment of our salvation. Paul expresses in his teaching his desire that we become in life what we already are in Christ. He teaches us not to live the physical Christian life by our own effort. He demands that we be filled with the Holy Spirit ***(Ephesians 5:18)***. He desires that the new man we put on be "after God" and that we would be created in righteousness and true holiness.

Righteousness means "right standing with God." True holiness simply means to be filled with the person of Christ, letting Him live His attitude, revelation, and relationship through us. In the light of this, religion is outside-in; Christianity is inside-out. To say it better, ***"but be [ye being] filled with the Holy Spirit" (Ephesians 5:18)***. Just as a clear glass filled to overflowing loses its identity to the crystal water, so we lose our identity to the Holy Spirit overflowing our bodies. What covers us is what we are.

Then Paul begins to deal with the Ephesians on the basis of their confession and conversation. In the ***25th verse***, he urges them to put away lying. He commands them to *"...speak truth with our neighbors."* In our confession we are not to say anything that would be an untruth. Our lives are to be a vital example of truth before our neighbors. Then he states that *"We are members, one of another."*

He then makes two unusual statements, which I believe we should consider very closely in this matter of "positive or negative confession." In ***Ephesians 4:26*** he says, ***"Be ye angry and sin not, let not the sun go down upon your wrath."*** God tells us we are not to sin when circumstances cause us to be angry. When we do allow anger to become wrath, Paul commands us not to allow the condition to remain when the sun goes down. In this regard, God is emphatic. We fan the fires of confusion by negative confession.

Back to Go

God says in ***Proverbs 17:14: "The beginning of strife is as when water first trickles (from a crack in a dam); therefore stop contention before it becomes worse and quarreling breaks out" (Amplified).*** In other words, *K.Y.M.S.*

Here God simply shares with us that "strife begins as a first trickle of water from a crack in a dam." He commands us to "stop the contention before it becomes worse and quarreling breaks out." God commands us not to continue to fan the flame. He is so emphatic on this point that He has provided praise in the Word of God as the means of handling it. He instructs us to stand in the midst of conflict, praising God for it. Again, this is a sign of spiritual maturity in the life of the individual. No matter what happens to you, God says you are to praise Him in all things ***(James 1:2-3)***. It is His way of developing maturity in you, the believer.

Look again at ***Ephesians 4:26***. Here God says: ***"Be ye angry and sin not; let not the sun go down on your wrath."*** Now, the ***27th verse*** is very short in the King James Version. It acts as an addendum to the ***26th verse***. It states, ***"neither give place to the devil."*** How do you give place to the devil? By remaining angry. The individual who is living on the basis of negative confession opens wide the door to Satan in his life. When a person becomes critical, caustic or bitter and harbors that condition in his own heart, the Bible declares he has given place to the devil. Satan has moved into his life and has destroyed all of God's Glory in that individual. Like the penalty in the board game "Monopoly" - you are sent back to "GO".

Again, look at these verses as they are together. ***"Be angry and sin not, let not the sun go down on your wrath. Neither give place to the devil," (Ephesians 4:26, 27).*** The quickest way for a Christian to destroy his relationship with God is by negative confession. God tells us that the individual who can control his tongue can control his whole body ***(James 3:2)***. When you are negative, critical and bitter and you make remarks through anger, you open your heart and life. In the process, Satan sweeps into your life.

God's command in the Amplified Version, in the ***27th verse***, says: ***"Leave no such room or foothold for the devil. Give no opportunity to him."*** God commands you not to allow hatred, bitterness or anger to remain in your heart ***(Philippians 3:13)***. The evident sign of maturity in the Christian's life is his ability to forgive and forget, and to praise in the midst of the storm. You are only as mature as the level of your praise in the midst of your conflicts. Always remember *K.Y.M.S. (Keep Your Mouth Shut!)*

Out of the Mouths of Babes

Now, go on to ***Ephesians 4:29***. The Amplified Bible reads:

> ***Let no foul or polluting language nor evil word, nor unwholesome or worthless talk (ever) come out of your mouth; but only such (speech) as is good and beneficial to the spiritual progress of others, as is fitting to the need and the occasion, that it may be a blessing and give grace (God's favor) to those who hear it.***

When I conduct revival meetings and come across a verse like this, I usually ask the congregation these questions before I expound on it: "Do you believe that the Bible is the inerrant Word of God? If so, please raise your hand. Do you believe it is divinely inspired, given by God, and that its Truths are pure Revelation and planned for the purpose of guiding men into the Will of God? Raise your hand."

For the most part, as far as I can remember, every hand has gone into the air. You say, "What is the purpose?" To get people— by their own admission—to stand with the Truth of the Word of God, especially around a verse such as this.

Let us study it carefully from the Amplified Bible. God's commandment begins: ***"Let no foul or polluting language..."*** What would the words ***"foul"*** and ***"polluting"*** mean? The dictionary gives us a clear understanding. It says of foul: "indecent; obscene, profane; as, foul language." Another word is "profanity." The evident sign of Satan's control in the life of the individual is the pattern of his speech. We shared with you an earlier verse that says, ***"Out of the abundance of the heart, the mouth speaketh."*** If an individual uses filthy language to accentuate either the negative or the positive aspects of his conversation, you can know from where it came. You can know also the condition of his spiritual life. His speech declares whether the condition of his heart is carnal or spiritual.

May I urge you, please, take no spiritual direction from any individual who uses filthy language. The purpose of filthy language is to accentuate either one's authority or strength or self-assuredness.

Those who study the mental corridors of human psychology know well that the individual who uses this kind of language feels he is incapable of adequately accentuating his own personality. It is a crutch. God commands the Christian to let his yea be yea, and his nay be nay ***(James 5:12)***. According to the Word of God, for the child of God to use cursing or any kind of negative exclamation to prove the position of his authority or personality is profane, obscene and indecent. What more can we say? Does that offend you? Are you offended, then, by the Word of God? Does God's Plan for the language He gave you disturb you? Do you feel that you have a better way of expressing things than He does? God's command is specific when it comes to obscenities. His answer to cursing is "No." The Christian who does it is spiritually separated from God. He is truly a "babe in Christ."

Give a Hoot - Don't Pollute

Pollution is one of the great problems in the world today. Someone has well said that this planet, in the next few years, will probably be buried in its own garbage. Waste management has become a multi-billion dollar industry. Researchers are desperately trying to find ways to recycle those things that humans cast aside as no longer useable. Pollution is a problem, not only to the human living standard, but also to the health of all living creatures.

Such is also true of our conversation. God uses the word ***"polluting"*** regarding the spoken word. It is a word that means to corrupt, to make unclean and impure, to desecrate. It simply means taking language that is pure and changing it into something that is filth. That describes the nature of negative confession. When you criticize another person's experience, you have polluted everything with your words. You have made a circumstance unclean, dirty and filthy. To destroy another individual's character by spoken word is to pollute. God's command to this is also an emphatic "No."

Going on in this verse, God states: ***"Nor evil word, nor unwholesome or worthless talk," (Ephesians 4:29).*** Again, the position of evil is the negative confession about another person. The individual who is critical of another person is spoken of literally in the Bible as one to be ***"pitied. "*** It also considers that person to be one who is speaking from "evil," as we will see later in ***James 3***. God's command concerning criticism is, again, an emphatic "No."

Then He goes on to say: ***"Nor unwholesome or worthless talk..."*** Now, the word ***"unwholesome"*** in this position is unusual but important. When we think of something unwholesome, we think of it as being harmful to the body or mind. It also means something is morally harmful or corrupt. It is from that position that we share this verse. People who criticize other people corrupt not only the people they are speaking about and to ***(James 3:4)***. They also destroy themselves. God emphasizes this in ***I Peter***, as we will see.

Look for a moment at what this does to the local church. The church as a body can be corrupted when people become critical of one another. You can walk into a church building where there is discord among the brethren and know inwardly that the Spirit is quenched. You sense the overwhelming atmospheric oppression, especially if you are to preach.

Conflict by criticism is Satan's greatest tool for destroying the ***"one accord"*** that must be present for God to minister His Grace. Negative confession destroys God's move to holiness in the lives of Christians. God's commandment concerning this position is also a resounding "No."

Finally, the Lord uses the words ***"worthless talk."*** In this case, criticism, according to the Word of God, is worthless. Again, gossip is anything that does not carry life or power. May I remind you that, if you desire to "walk" with God, you have only two ways to speak about another person. You may speak only in prayer or in praise: praying for them if they have a problem; praising God for them in their victories. God sees your being negative toward an individual's character or toward a situation as totally worthless. If you see something in a person's life that you feel should not be, instead of sharing it with someone else in a critical way, God commands you to pray.

Also, here the word ***"worthless"*** is the same as the word ***"naughty"*** we saw in ***Proverbs 6:12*** and ***17:4***. This, again, is from the Hebrew word "Beliyaal," which takes its root from the word "Belial." This is the word for Satan. We can paraphrase this by saying that he who has ***"worthless talk"*** is full of the devil. I did not say it; God did.

Now, for the rest of this verse - here God says that these things are never, ever to ***"Come out of your mouth."*** Then He qualifies the kind of confession that we are to have. ***"But only such (speech) as is good and beneficial to the spiritual progress of others," (Ephesians 4:29, Amplified).*** Now, what does that mean? Very simply, the only way we can talk about another individual is through what? Through prayer or praise! Criticism will bring another person down. You see, our conversation must be in Christ ***(I Peter 3:16)***. We must declare only that which is beneficial to the spiritual progress of others. We must either speak to the individual that which will help him in his walk with Christ, or we must speak to

God about him to accomplish the same end.

God gives you no opening for criticism under any circumstance. It is one thing to admonish an individual to his face. It is something else to criticize that person to another individual who has absolutely nothing to do with what is going on. God commands us to speak only that which benefits and helps another person to walk with Jesus Christ. That is only what is "fitting to the need and the occasion."

God is so emphatic about the spoken word that He even qualifies the kind of conversation or confession we are to have. I urge you to try something here that works. Look for something good in everything. Then speak it, if possible, to another. That is the most incredibly healing thing that you can do, not only for the person or situation you are addressing but also for what it does to you as an individual. God will bless you for being this kind of person.

We must learn that we are not to speak until we are spoken through. If we commit our "confession" to Christ, He will order our speech according to His will. In a beautiful prayer verse out of the book of Job we read, ***"We cannot order our speech by reason of darkness..." (Job 37:19)***. The ***"darkness"*** comes from not knowing the mind or the will of God. So we must seek it in order to pray and speak according to His will.

The individual who coordinates his life with the operation of Christ's will and purpose for him will break himself of ever speaking without God's flow through his life. When he allows the Lord to deliver him from a critical tongue, he will enter into a greater walk with Christ. We will emphasize this even more as we go further into the study of controlling the lips.

Now, in our journey through this verse, let us take one step further in studying what God emphasizes concerning the spoken word. Again, He tells us not to speak anything except what brings spiritual progress to others and fits the need and the occasion of the individual.

God qualifies our speech in the rest of ***Ephesians 4:29, Amplified*** by stating: ***"that it may be a blessing and give grace (God's favor) to those who hear it."*** These lines include a word whose meaning is almost beyond the limited expression of human language. It is a word we must understand, not by reason, but by spiritual revelation. That is the word ***"grace."*** I have done a word study on this precious expression God has given us. We have even placed a message on our monthly tape ministry titled "Grace." Nevertheless, I do not feel that we are able even to begin to touch the proverbial "hem of the garment" in the true meaning of this beautiful word.

Grace, as simply as I can describe it, is God's flow of the Life of Christ to and through a Christian's life. The usual understanding of this word is God's "unmerited favor." This means God gives us more than we merit or deserve. That, however, is a mere grain of sand standing beside the pile that would be made if we were to crush all the galaxies into small particles. That description is still not great enough to explain God's matchless grace to us as believers. However, through grace comes unlimited divine power in our life. That power is so flowing and is so real that a person comes, in his spirit, face-to-face with the living Lord Jesus. In the process of facing Christ, he is spoken to and through by His matchless Person. As God speaks grace through us, we speak His grace to others.

God's Heart is Broken

In the light of this, what is God's command to us? He wants our speech to be so ordered and so placed in Jesus Christ that when we do make a statement before men it will be a blessing to them. It will "give grace (God's favor) to those who hear it." This includes everything that we say. There is no room for criticism. There is no room to be caustic or bitter. There is no room for anger. In fact, sustained anger moves God completely out of the situation and places the devil in complete control.

Oh Why, Oh Why, Oh Why?

For several years now, we have used the broadcast media to preach the Gospel. Through television and radio we speak the message of God's grace. When we do so, we invite people to write us of their needs for prayer. Because of this, we have received letters from those whom God has blessed through the messages, as well as from those who have deep needs.

I shall never forget opening an envelope one morning with several dollars inside. Enclosed was a letter I had to read several times to get its full impact. The sentences were simply written. It was from a heart that was speaking from two positions: one in brokenness and the other in victory. According to the letter a young mother was home one day when her brother came by to visit. When he pulled up in front of the house, she walked out to his pick-up. In the course of their conversation, she did not notice her one-year-old daughter who had been toddling around in the yard suddenly slip through the gate. As the mother turned to go back into the house, this precious young child wandered in front of the truck. When the brother engaged the gear and gave this instrument life by giving gas to its motor, he suddenly felt something under his wheel. The mother screamed, he stopped, and there underneath the vehicle was the little girl who no longer sustained life in her body. She was gone.

After relating these events, the mother went on to share what Christ had meant to her life in those tragic days. She shared how friends had stood by her and prayed with her. At the end of the letter she made the statement (in essence), “Even through all of this, it’s all right.” I went to the community of this family some weeks later to conduct a series of meetings and met the woman and her husband. Again, they assured me that Jesus Christ was the strength of their lives and that they had victory in their hearts. In listening to them, I knew that within them was God’s Grace and Peace. He truly was sufficient ***(II Corinthians 12:9)***.

You say, “Brother Bonner, why would you share that at this point in this writing?” Very simply, to express to you a meaning that you must grasp in order to understand what God says in this next verse. The illustration is this: Suppose a mother, seeing her child wander into the street, pursues that precious bundle of life. Before she can reach the child, a truck careens around the corner, hits the child and ends his life. The mother then falls upon her knees, picks up the lifeless form of that child to whom she had given life through her own body. She cradles it to her chest and buries her face in its rumpled clothing and screams out, “Oh why, oh why?” You say, again, “What is the point?” When a Christian criticizes another individual; when he becomes caustic, bitter or evil in his speech regarding them; when he becomes foul in his language, or polluting in his statements of another person’s character or circumstance, that person crowds the Holy Spirit over to the corner of his spirit. There the heartbroken Holy Spirit cries out, “Oh why, oh why, oh why?”

For, you see, in the beginning lines of ***Ephesians 4:30***, after the commandment against negative confession in the prior verse, God says through Paul, ***“And do not grieve the Holy Spirit.”*** How do we grieve the Spirit of God? With our mouths. How do we grieve God’s precious Spirit and person? With our confessions. With what we say. We vex

Him - we offend Him - we sadden Him. When we sadden Him, we have brought grief to the heart of God within our person. That is, with our lips we break the heart of God. He feels the same grief as that mother who lost her child.

Grow Up

The evident sign of growth in the life of the Christian is the ability to take everything anyone says about him or does to him and praise the Lord for it. The sign of immaturity is to react and be critical, caustic, bitter or negative. Look at ***verse 30*** again where God declares we are *"not to grieve the Holy Spirit of God."* This statement is God's conclusion to all that He says in the prior verses. We grieve Him with our confession.

We see this further established in ***Ephesians 4:31*** and ***32***, particularly in the Amplified.

> ***Let all bitterness and indignation and wrath (passion, rage, bad temper) and resentment (anger, animosity) and quarreling (brawling, clamor, contention) and slander (evil speaking, abusive or blasphemous language) be banished from you, with all malice (spite, ill will or baseness of any kind). And become useful and helpful and kind to one another, tenderhearted (compassionate, understanding, loving hearted), forgiving one another [readily and freely] as God in Christ forgave you.***

God instructs us on what we are to do. We are to take ***"bitterness and indignation and wrath, resentment, quarreling, slander"*** out of our person. Notice that, for the most part, these all have to do with confession. It is that which originates from the heart and proceeds through our mouths. He qualifies our negative response as passion. This is the spoken word literally spawned by rage. It is the inner conflict of personal character that becomes uncontrollable. It is the destroyer, working to destroy the believer from within.

He then goes on to say, "bad temper," which expresses itself as negative confession. From there, He speaks of ***"anger and animosity."*** These are violent explosions within the personality that usually find their outlet through spoken words. All of this climaxes into ***"quarreling,"*** which is, again, spoken words. This is being so inflexibly negative with another individual that you lose all rationality or reason. You begin to fuss and fight. You are out of control. Therefore, your speech does not have the quality of Christ in it. You declare your rights, your place, or your position in the subject, circumstance or situation. Grace, at that moment, is not your spiritual posture. Your character is not the quality of Christ. You produce all this by the spoken word.

After the ***"quarreling"*** come the results of not controlling your tongue. ***"Brawling, clamor, contention"*** all follow closely on its heels. Again, these could have to do with positional speech, as well as physical action. Pride and insecurity cause you to try to assert your "rights" within your own individual person. For the most part you express all these heart eruptions by the spoken word.

Kicked Off the Throne

From here, God goes on to say: ***"and slander (evil-speaking, abusive or blasphemous language)."*** Do you see God's direction here? ***"Slander"*** means you develop in your mind the negative aspects of another person's character or circumstance. Webster's dictionary describes it as "the expression of damaging or malicious opinions." In other words, gossip. God says this evil speaking ***"grieves"*** the Holy Spirit. Therein lies God's definition of slander. It is ***"abusive or blasphemous language."*** We can explain this simply as "cursing." Christians who do these things do not walk with God. They do not hear from God. God does not flow through their lives under any circumstance.

Here God declares His position on criticism. He says to make sure it is ***"banished from you."*** The word ***"banish"*** is not used a great deal in today's language. It is similar in meaning to the word "abdication," removing one's own self from a position of authority such as abdicating a throne. However, we use the word ***"banish"*** to express the forced physical removal of a person in control. God says we are to banish these areas of Satan's control from our life. More simply put, we are to take away his power by keeping our mouths shut. Again, "He who controls his lips can control his whole body."

God says there is no place in the life of the individual for ***"malice."*** Here, in conjunction with the word ***"malice,"*** He uses the words ***"spite, ill will, or baseness of any kind."*** Do you understand that, in connection with the prior verses in this chapter, all of this qualifies as the area of spoken word? Can you see how important it is that we control our speech? God is so emphatic in these areas that He even connects these confessions with the way we are to live. In ***Ephesians 4:32*** He commands us to:

> ***And be ye kind one to another, tenderhearted, forgiving one another, even as God for Christ's sake hath forgiven you, (KJV).***

> ***become useful and helpful and kind to one another, tenderhearted (compassionate, understanding, loving-hearted),***

forgiving one another (readily and freely), as God in Christ forgave you. (Amplified)

We have analyzed these verses word by word so we can understand their complete meaning. Now we can state that most of these things are to be found in one area of our life - in our spoken word. Once you bring your mouth into control, then your body will follow.

Someone has well said, "What is in the well comes up in the bucket." Scripturally that is, ***"Out of the abundance of the heart, the mouth speaketh."*** If you really want to know who you are and what you are in the kingdom of God, listen to what you say. Better still, "Listen with your heart to what you like to listen to with your ear." That will express to you the level of your heart's walk with Christ.

Focus Questions

"Never Listen to Negative Criticism or Gossip"

1. Paul in his writing to the Church of Ephesus dealt very severely with the area of negative confession. How did he tell them to overcome negative confession?

2. Negative confession fans the fires of "confusion." What does ***Proverbs 17:14*** tell us about how negative confession fans the fires of "confusion?"

3. What verse tells us who the author of confusion is? How does he operate in your life to bring confusion?

4. From ***Ephesians 4:29*** in the Amplified Bible, what do the words foul and polluting mean?

5. What does the Word of God tell us about the meaning and impact of criticism?

6. Very simply stated, the only way we can talk about another individual is through prayer or praise. How can we accomplish this?

7. What does the word "grace" mean? How does your answer compare to the dictionary definition? In the light of these definitions are we giving 'grace' to each other when we choose to speak negatively or critically of one another?

8. In ***Ephesians 4:29-30***, God commands against negative confession and then says, ***"And do not grieve the Holy Spirit of God."*** How do we grieve the spirit of God?

9. What does ***Ephesians 4:31-32*** tell us to do to overcome negative confession? How do we do it? Write out ***Ephesians 4:32*** and make it your prayer for yourself.

10. From a practical viewpoint, what you say reveals to the whole world what you are on the inside. Assess your own confession. Based on what you say, who are you?

Understand we are talking about your practice. If you are In Christ, meaning you are a born again Christian, you are all of the things Ephesians chapter one says that you are, these are positional truths. And because of who we are in Christ (our position), the instructions in God's Word are what we are to "practice." In other words "how we are to live, in the light of who we are." - Editor

CHAPTER FIVE

I'm Too Fat

James 3, in the Amplified states:

Not many (of you) should become teachers (self-constituted censors and reprovers of others), my brethren, for you know that we (teachers) will be judged by a higher standard and with greater severity (than other people)—Thus we assume the greater accountability and the more condemnation. For we all often stumble and fall and offend in many things. And if any one does not offend in speech—never says the wrong things—he is a fully developed character and a perfect man, able to control his whole body and to curb his entire nature. If we set bits in the horses' mouths to make them obey us, we can turn their whole bodies about. Likewise, look at the ships, though they are so great and are driven by rough winds, they are steered by a very small rudder wherever the impulse of the helmsman determines. Even so, the tongue is a little member, and it can boast of great things. See how much wood or how great a forest a tiny spark can set ablaze! And the tongue (is) a fire. (The tongue is a) world of wickedness set among our members, contaminating and depraving the whole body and setting on fire the wheel of birth—the cycle of man ‘s nature being itself ignited by hell (Gehenna). For every kind of beast and bird, of

reptile and sea animal, can be tamed and has been tamed by human genius (nature). But the human tongue can be tamed by no man. It is (an undisciplined, irreconcilable) restless evil full of death-bringing poison. With it we bless the Lord and Father, and with it we curse men who were made in God's likeness! Out of the same mouth come forth blessing and cursing. These things, my brethren, ought not to be so. Does a fountain send forth (simultaneously) from the same opening fresh water and bitter? Can a fig tree, my brethren, bear olives, or a grapevine figs? Neither can a salt spring furnish fresh water. Who is there among you who is wise and intelligent? Then let him by his noble living show forth his (good) works with the (unobtrusive) humility (which is the proper attribute) of true wisdom. But if you have bitter jealousy (envy) and contention (rivalry, selfish ambition) in your hearts, do not pride yourselves on it and thus be in defiance of and false to the Truth. This (superficial) wisdom is not such as comes down from above, but is earthly, unspiritual (animal), even devilish (demoniacal). For wherever there is jealousy (envy) and contention (rivalry and selfish ambition), there will also be confusion (unrest, disharmony, rebellion) and all sorts of evil and vile practices. But the wisdom from above is first of all pure (undefiled); then it is peaceloving, courteous (considerate, gentle). (It is willing to) yield to reason, full of compassion and good fruits; it is wholehearted and straightforward, impartial and unfeigned—free from doubts, wavering and insincerity. And the harvest of righteousness (of conformity to God's will in thought and deed) is (the fruit of the seed) sown in peace by those who work for and make peace—in themselves and in others, (that is) that peace

which means concord (agreement, harmony) between individuals, with undisturbedness, in a peaceful mind free from fears and agitating passions and moral conflicts.

In ***James 3***, we find one of the strongest positions that God takes on the spoken word. Here, by inspiration He gives the reader His adamant stand about the control of the tongue. In these verses, He declares the strength of the tongue and its ability to build or to destroy. God says so much concerning this subject in this chapter that we will speak only to those verses that describe most strongly God's purposes in our speech. However, I do urge the reader to study this chapter over and over for himself. Through it, he may learn God's declared position concerning the spoken word. As we have said several times in this volume, God commands us literally, not to speak until we have been spoken through.

Nobody's Perfect

Let us begin with ***James 3:2***:

"For we all often stumble and fall and offend in many things. And if any one does not offend in speech—never says the wrong things—he is a fully developed character and a perfect man, able to control his whole body and to curb his entire nature.

On several occasions, I have had people ask me how they can get rid of a certain bondage in their lives. For the most part, this question concerns their being overweight. My stock answer to that person is, *"Keep your mouth shut."* Now, I know that in essence that statement may sound trite. It may even be a little harsh. However, I do not mean it to be so. God says in His Word that the individual who can control his tongue can control his whole body. When someone says to me, "I have no control over certain areas of my life or my body," they have simply said, "I cannot control my confession."

Examine ***verse 2*** in that light. God tells us, ***"All often stumble and fall and offend in many things."*** Now, of course, the stock answer to these problems is: "We are all human - we have our faults," or the classic answer, "Nobody's perfect." I agree that we are subject to Satan's ***"wiles"*** in this. Also, we are sometimes victims of circumstances. However, as Christians, the myriad of conflicts and blessings in our lives should develop our character and personalities as we go through them in Christ.

Most often, however, these conflicts produce insecurities and inferiorities that we must constantly cleanse by daily dying to self. Then, in the process of daily crucifixion, we take on the resurrected nature of Jesus Christ ***(Galatians 2:20).*** This is the only process that overcomes the deep negative habit-traits and patterns in our lives. Christ has to consume and control our lives. It is our choice to relinquish or hold on to our own control. When we relinquish control to Christ we are less likely to ***"stumble and fall and offend in many things."***

Speaking without Love

God continues by saying you must come to a certain position in your spoken word. He states, ***"And if anyone does not offend in speech."*** Now, what does the word ***"offend"*** mean in this statement? There are several meanings to the word. The best in this case is "to create resentment, anger, or displeasure; give offense." It also means "to hurt the feelings of, or to cause to feel resentful, angry, or displeased." It means also "to insult."

With these definitions in mind, based not only on the dictionary's position, but also from the Greek word, let us speak of it again. The Scripture says: ***"If anyone does not offend in speech..."*** This means never be caustic, critical or bitter or unkind toward another individual in your spoken word. Please understand the gravity of this. When a Christian is critical in this carnal, baby state, he separates himself from God.

Look at what God says next. If ***"... he does not offend in speech - never says the wrong things, he is a fully developed character, and a perfect man..."*** Here God gets to the point. He declares this Christian has a ***"fully developed character."*** Let us look at it this way. The word "develop" means to take something to the end of its position, such as to express more fully and in greater detail. For example, research and development departments take a project to its very end in order to get to its maximum position.

The individual who has learned to control his speech, according to the Word of God, is being fully developed by God's Spirit into the nature of Jesus Christ. The nature of Christ is not negativity. The nature of Christ is life. Through Him flows abundant life. So, as the individual grows in grace, he learns to control his speech. He never says the wrong things. He finds that he is never critical, caustic, or bitter in his statements. He never speaks orally the anger he might feel inside. God's Word teaches that individual is being developed into the nature and flow-through ministry of Christ.

God says this Christian is a fully developed character. The word "develop" means, again, to take something to the end of its position, such as in a business or corporation. Projects begin with extensive research and development by individuals. They continue to work with the idea until they can manufacture it into a product. The idea is now fully developed. In this same manner, the product developed in ***James 3*** is the moral strength, the self-discipline and the fortitude of Christ. Such is the nature of the individual who is so consumed by Christ that his words are ***"developed"*** into the person of Christ. As he grows in grace, he takes on the character of Christ in his life. He loses his critical tongue by seeing the individual who has been overtaken in a fault through the eyes of Christ ***(Galatians 6:1)***.

There are proper times to be adamant in a circumstance. In the course of my lifetime as a preacher of the Gospel message, I have had to take many strong stands in preaching. There has been the quality of genuine righteous indignation in certain matters; however, these did not consume or control me. On the contrary, I experienced these feelings because of the person of Christ working through my heart. When I gave such a message by God's power in love, it always brought forth good fruit. Then, on other occasions, I have preached in anger, knowing a truth to be truth, and through carnal flesh, I adamantly presented the message. I have hurt people in doing so. God commands us to *"speak the truth in love"* ***(Ephesians 4:15)***. I have begged His forgiveness many times in this regard. It always happened when my "busy-ness" with ministry became more important than my prayer life.

Perfection in Christ

Again, He says: ***"... he is a fully developed character and a perfect man, able to control his whole body and to curb his entire***

nature." Now what, specifically, does the Lord mean by this? It is very simple: there is none perfect but Christ. However, in this case, the word means "to be perfected." The individual who learns to control his speech, who never says the wrong things, who is never critical of another person, who never speaks in anger regardless of the experience of his own heart, God says, is "being perfected." Of course, the word "perfection," at this point, simply means that God is changing him "into the nature of Christ." Jesus, Who is perfection, becomes more and more the center and force of this person's life.

Check your speech to know where you are with Christ, for ***"Out of the abundance of the heart the mouth speaketh."*** You are what you say - what comes out of your mouth declares the very person you are with Christ, with the world, and with your attitude toward yourself. Your words are power, as we have already seen in ***Proverbs: "Life and death are in the power of the tongue."*** So, the individual who can control his tongue never says an unkind thing. He is being perfected daily into the nature of Christ. Not only that, there is nothing else in that person's life that controls him. God goes so far as to say that you will be able to curb your entire nature if you can control your tongue.

The word "nature" is related to the word "natural." You who have studied the Bible know that the Scripture teaches that the "natural man" cannot walk in the fullness of Christ. He does not know what it is to be filled with the person of Jesus and to be established in His will. He knows nothing of being disciplined to the point that his nature is curbed or controlled. Discipline is the coordination of the inner personality causing it to work within certain guidelines. The Christian who can control his speech can be brought into this blessing.

Is there something about your own life that you do not like? Perhaps there is an area within that you know God has burdened you about, and you want desperately to overcome it. God teaches that if you curb your tongue, you can control any area of your life. The position of the verse is very simple. The person who can control what he says will have nothing else dominating his life. God always says what He means.

The Tongue is a Fire

In the next several verses of this chapter in ***James***, God talks about the physical tongue itself within the body of the individual. Even though it is small, it sets the course of a person's entire life-style. Another way to say it is, "You are what you say." He speaks of bits in the horse's mouth. Men design these to make the horse turn at the rider's command so it will go in the direction that he wants. God speaks of the very small helm that causes the ship to take the desired course or direction of the individual in control of the rudder. God purposes in these illustrations to show the reader that ***"even so, the tongue is a little member, and it can boast of great things. See how much wood or how great a forest a tiny spark can set ablaze."***

Loose Lips Sink Ships

This reminds me of a phrase I heard as a very young boy during the Second World War. We lived in Houston, Texas, the home of the third largest port in America with a large shipbuilding yard nearby.

Many ships found themselves at portside being loaded with essential war materials. Houston had many people who were on the side of our enemy, the Axis powers, and sought information about sailings, cargo, and destinations. Therefore, the government posted the phrase

"Loose lips sink ships" on all piers, plants, warehouses, and places of staging as the equipment was assigned to its destination. One word could destroy many lives: both on the ship itself, and at its destination. Such is the power of the tongue that is not controlled. A tiny spark can cause a raging fire of destruction and death. When this happens Satan wins again. The answer: *K.Y.M.S.*

Then, in the fifth verse, God states that one word spoken can completely devastate or destroy a character, a nature or a circumstance. It is a spark that completely sets a forest ablaze. How many times has the critical Christian destroyed a life and, at the same time, burned up his works in heaven? How tragic!

Dry Bones

In the sixth verse, He takes us into one of the deepest doctrinal areas based on the power of the tongue itself. Let us look at it:

> ***And the tongue (is) a fire. (The tongue is a world of wickedness set among our members, contaminating and depraving the whole body and setting on fire the wheel of birth - the cycle of man's nature - being itself ignited by hell (Gehenna). (James 3:6, Amplified)***

As we have stated previously, the tongue is a power. To quote ***Proverbs 18:21, "Death and life are in the power of the tongue."*** I have personally seen the spoken word actually bind or loose a circumstance in a person's life. I believe that a person can speak a curse by allowing hateful words to exit from his critical heart. In the spiritualist world of witchcraft, this is the foundation of all of their belief in the casting of spells. They use incantations to bring in their defeated demon spirits to possess or control. Yes, this is biblical.

I believe God establishes this fact in this verse. I have seen people make critical statements of other people and bind their lives. I have seen others bind themselves by making negative statements that would eventually set into motion circumstances that would bring conflict to that person's character, physical being or life direction.

Those who are constantly critical of themselves release power for Satan to use against them. An example of this is: "The older I get, the worse I feel," or, "I just can't remember anything anymore," or "I know this is going to be a bad day." This list could go on and on. I think these examples are sufficient to make my point.

Also, I would like to add here that I have seen many who are physically ill bring themselves to that infirmity by negative confession. Arthritis is a good example of this. I have found that many who have this disease are people who are or have been constantly negative in their attitudes.

However, let us take ***verse 6*** apart and see its power. God says: ***"The tongue is a fire and it is a world of wickedness set among our members."*** Of course, the "world" has to do with a specific position by itself. You have heard someone say: "I live in my own little world." He means that, as an individual, he has developed his own life-style and does not want anyone else to enter into it. That person is a rebel, a maverick, and one who has set himself apart or pulled into himself. This is a sickness in itself. God speaks of the tongue as being exactly the same way. He states that it can actually set the course of human history or human nature. The tongue is an independent, separate world.

Not only that, it will contaminate and deprave the whole body. Now what does that mean? What you say is what you are. People who constantly criticize are those who are perpetually ill. They have physical maladies and spiritual problems in their own lives.

Arthritis is an illness of the bones and sockets drying out, and criticism can cause the bones to dry. ***Proverbs 17:22 states: "A happy heart is a good medicine and a cheerful mind works healing, but a broken spirit dries the bones" (Amplified).*** I am not saying that all arthritics are critical, for many have genetic, organic arthritis. However, there are scriptural positions that establish that the curse of criticism can generate physical maladies. The tongue itself can contaminate the whole physical body. It can destroy it. The person who is chronically negative in his confession is also chronically ill in his physical being or his personality. He is the kind of individual who can hardly wait for you to get through telling him how bad you feel, so he can tell you how bad he feels. You must have a positive confession.

Never "harangue" other people with your negative feelings. Praise God for them - praise God in them - and most of all, praise God for your position. Praise God for your person, thanking Him for the circumstances you are in. In the process of praise, you bring the Holy Spirit in to take your burden. He fills you with joy and His grace becomes sufficient. Learn to control your confession. Better yet, learn to allow Christ to control you. Learn not to let Satan consume you by being negative. The speech itself, or words emitting from your mouth, can contaminate and "deprave" your whole body. Satan uses them against you.

The Frog in the Pot

God continues in ***verse 6*** by saying: ***"... setting on fire of the wheel of birth - the cycle of man's nature - being ignited by hell***

(Gehenna)." Man's nature is depraved and, sadly enough, it is constantly becoming more depraved. Check his conversation. Check your conversation. Check the media. Nothing is sacred anymore.

Let me give you an illustration. If, ten years ago, they had shown on television what they are showing now; if you had heard the words sung or spoken, the insinuations, the bedroom scenes now on "prime-time" television; there would have been open demonstrations against the networks. "Do you think it would have been that bad, Brother Bonner?" I believe there would have been people up in arms over this situation.

However, we have been fed strychnine (compromise) in such small doses that it has collected in our bone marrow. That slow process eventually will take the life of a person. Today, this country has almost died from permissiveness and apathy. We have become weakened inside. We just do not care so we now accept the demon possessed lifestyles as normal. We are sick unto death, and God's judgment is upon us. We must change our confession to prayer. We must humble ourselves before we can make that change in order to be heard by God ***(II Corinthians 7:14).***

Several years ago, scientists did an experiment to demonstrate physical reactions to circumstance. They found that if you took a frog and put it into a pot of cold water and placed it over a flame, letting the heat increase very slowly, eventually the frog would cook and die. However, they also found that if you heated the water to that temperature and then dropped the frog in, it would immediately jump out, thereby protecting itself.

A recent incident shows this can even happen to humans. A man and his wife bought a special unit similar to a heated tub. They had it installed in their home and were in the water, basking in its heat, anticipating its medicinal remedies. However, the thermostat broke, and they stood it as long as they could, thinking that it was supposed to be that hot. Both of these people sustained such burns that they died.

This is what has happened to our country, based on its confessions. Filth has so consumed us that we have become used to it. We are a nation of negative people with little fences built around our relationships, commanding others not to come in. Our whole world is being ignited, inflamed with the fires of hell, by spoken word. How tragic the devastating consequences!

You say, "What can stop it?" The opposite of negative is positive. Positive confession is, ***"In everything giving thanks,"*** and ***"Praising God for all things."*** No matter what people do to you, do not speak an unkind word, but praise God in everything. Let Jesus Christ be Lord of your life, and Lord of your lips, totally and completely. Once you have done this, you will enter into His transformed life and experience "joy unspeakable" and be full of His glory.

Going on in ***James chapter 3***, God refers to other things that can be tamed. The genius of man has made him able to capture nearly every living thing and bring it under his control. By contrast though, here God states in the ***eighth verse: "the human tongue can be tamed by no man."*** He declares: ***"It is a restless undisciplined, irreconcilable evil full of deadly poison."*** Now this, very clearly, is God's description of the human tongue.

Shape Up or Ship Out

We have tried to share with you the fact that God is completely against negative confession in any form. He declares that we must control our speech. He demands that we control our tongue. We must be in control of everything that comes out of our mouths. However, since He also declares, ***"but the tongue no man can tame,"*** we must consciously submit our speech to His control. We cannot control it ourselves. What we say is really what we are. Our whole person or personality can be wrapped up in the words that proceed out of our mouths. When we allow Him to control our mouths, then His personality will be evident in every part of our lives.

The word ***"undisciplined"*** means that there is an absence of Spirit-discipline, Spirit-control. For instance, take an individual whose dress is immaculate, whose complete demeanor is that of quality and whose character is of complete control. This individual presents a striking picture of poise and personality, and yet in conversation, he becomes critical, caustic and bitter. He tears down the character of another person's life. I think this illustrates basically what God is saying. Not only is that individual undisciplined, but he is also irreconcilable. Nothing you can tell him will change his mind. He is hate personified. God says he is restless in his own person. He is filled with evil, but most of all, he is ***"... full of death-bringing poison."***

Now, those who heard this in the time of God's original inspiration of the book of ***James*** knew that the ***"death-bringing poison"*** could come from something taken or from an encounter with a spider or snake. What God was saying literally to them was they should fear the person who is bitter, caustic and critical as much as they feared poison as an instrument of death. How much more must God say in His Word to make the individual who is critical change what he is saying or what he is doing? "But," you say, "I'm a Christian, and I know I'm critical, but I just can't help it." Yes, you can. Or rather, Jesus can. In fact, the level of your walk with Christ is based on the level of your conversation.

Once again we see that ***"out of the abundance of the heart, the mouth speaketh,"*** or "you are what you say." Most of all, it means shape up, or you have already shipped out - spiritually.

Is God a Fool?

With these things in mind, let us go on to the ***ninth verse of James 3***. ***"With it we bless the Lord and Father, and with it we curse men who were made in God's likeness!"*** Here He states that, at one moment, we bless God and the next moment, we curse men. Then we receive the declaration that all men are made in God's likeness. Now, we have already shared out of ***Ephesians 4*** what God says about cursing and the use of negative statements to accentuate bitter or boastful feelings. This is actually what cursing is. Cursing is the verbal expression of inward insecurity. It shows a person's inability to express himself in such a way as to have confidence he is being received and understood. Therefore, such an individual must accentuate his conversation with curse words. What a tragedy! That individual shows ignorance more than dominance or authority.

I must emphasize once more, God gave us the tongue for one reason: to bless Him. When we curse men, we curse God, for man is made in His likeness. Take it one step further. Can you imagine, based on this verse, what it is to curse God? Men use phrases to accentuate their positions that involve taking God's name in vain. When you take God's name in vain to declare your disdain of another individual, you are not really cursing that individual as much as you are cursing God. You are saying, as you curse that person, "God, you are a fool. You made that individual. Why don't you damn him?" I am sorry if the strength of that offends you, but it is absolute truth from the Word of God. People who curse are sick in their soul: they should be pitied.

Sweet and Bitter Water

Now, let us further examine the Scripture and see if a Christian has a right to be negative. Looking at ***verse 10*** we find: ***"Out of the same mouth come forth blessing and cursing. These things, my brethren, ought not to be so."*** Then, from ***verse 11: "Does a fountain send forth (simultaneously) from the same opening fresh water and bitter?"***

Here God shows us that if out of a person's mouth there come forth blessing and cursing, that person is unspiritual and inconsistent. This reveals the weakness of the Christian's walk in Christ. As we shared earlier in this writing, do not take any kind of spiritual instruction from a person who is negative toward another individual ***(I John 2:11)***. By the same token, receive no spiritual instruction from the individual who uses foul or polluting language. Why? Because he receives no revelation. His Christian experience is all hearsay, something he has heard or read, that he spreads on to you. There is no Holy Spirit-given revelation in the life of that person.

God says it best in ***James 1:26, 27*** in the Amplified:

> ***If anyone thinks himself to be religious - piously observant of the external duties of his faith - and does not bridle his tongue, but deludes his own heart, this person's religious service is worthless (future, barren). External religious worship (religion as it is expressed in outward acts) that is pure and unblemished in the sight of God the Father is this: to visit and help and care for the orphans and widows in their affliction and need, and to keep oneself unspotted and uncontaminated from the world.***

Here is God's true test of your relationship to His will. It is not what you say, but what God is doing through you by the work of the Holy Spirit. Please never forget that He is in you to continue the work of Christ through you.

God proves an old adage here in these verses. That is, if you speak a lie enough times, there will come a time when others receive it as truth. How many of us talk ourselves into a ministry with which God has nothing to do? Critical people delude their own hearts while doing nothing of the Kingdom's true work. That is a great tragedy. Your words set the course of your life. God commands you to bridle your tongue. Again, *K.Y.M.S.*

"How do you know that, Brother Bonner?" Look at the Scriptures. In ***James 3:11***, God states, ***"Does a fountain send forth (simultaneously) from the same opening fresh water and bitter?"*** Absolutely not. You see, if a fountain is bitter, that which comes out of that fountain is going to be bitter. However, a person can present it as sweet water by clouding over the bitterness so it does not retain its taste. However, it is still poison.

This perfectly illustrates the critical Christian. One moment he speaks good things about God. Then, the next moment he criticizes people. You know immediately that the sweet things he says of God do not originate by the Spirit of God and do not come from the flow of God. His confession is nothing in the world but saccharin added to bitter water. It is false and unreal. Take no spiritual instruction from any person who is critical or who curses. Were they consumed by God, they would speak by His Spirit: there would be true sweet water.

By Their Fruits

God continues to emphasize this in the next verse when He reveals the fact that ***"...a fig tree cannot bear olives."*** There has never been success in grafting a shoot from one tree to the other when they do not share the same genetic origin. It cannot sustain life. Its total DNA make-up is different.

In the same manner, certain trees produce fruit that is beautiful to the outward eye but when ingested brings death. Let us suppose such a tree with its poisoned fruit wanted to present fruit people would accept as good. It begins by designing a new outward skin over one of its products, but the essence of the fruit does not change because the life does not change. Someone comes along and says, "That fruit looks good (or in the case of confession, 'sounds good'). I know these other berries are poison, but this one looks good to the eye. Its texture on the outside looks edible; therefore, I will eat it and not touch the other poison berries of the tree." In the course of the experience the person dies. (In the case of confession, the death is spiritual.) What has happened? The tree has presented false fruit. ***"A tree is known by his fruit" (Matthew 12:33).***

Squeeze a Lemon

In ***John 15:1-7***, the fruit of the Christian is not another Christian. The fruit of the Christian is Jesus Christ Himself produced through that person. We are the branches, and Jesus produces Himself through us as a branch ***(John 15:5-7).*** When He does, people partaking of the fruit of our lives do not look at the branch and say, "Oh, wonderful branch." They look at our fruit and declare of the Vine, "Oh, glorious Vine." Who is the Vine? Jesus Christ! Therefore, people who are bitter or caustic or critical or speak negative words or innuendoes are nothing in the world but bitter fruit. They produce of the branch (themselves) and not of the Vine (Jesus Christ). No matter how the person clothes the fruit, it still carries death. You always get out of the well what is in it. Or, again, what comes up in the bucket is what is down in the well. Another way of saying it (as a friend of mine states often), "When you squeeze a lemon, you get what is in it." You are known by your fruit, especially when you are squeezed!

If you would really like to know what kind of character you have, don't listen to yourself when things are going well, but listen to what comes out of you when you have been "squeezed." That's what you really are. Under pressure, what proceeds out of your mouth is your true character. You say, "I don't like that." Regardless of that, it is truth. Change your confession from the inside. Let Jesus become Lord of your life and learn not to speak until spoken through. God says, in ***Galatians 5:1: "Stand fast therefore in the liberty wherewith Christ hath made us free and be not entangled again with the yoke of bondage."***

Also, memorize ***Proverbs 16:1*** in the Amplified Bible. It states: ***"The plans of the mind and orderly thinking belong to man, but from the Lord comes the (wise) answer of the tongue."*** In essence, this says we are not to speak until spoken through. Man can devise according to his own mental ability and the directions of his own mind, but from God comes the ***"wise answer of the tongue."*** If you do not like the way you are; if you hate what comes out of your mouth—your criticism, your causticity or bitterness—then you need to commit your life to Christ. He can and will change you. But you must bring your confession under His control. You must bind your words to Christ's control. You must allow Christ to deliver you.

In the King James Version of ***James 3:11***, God says: ***"Does a fountain send forth at the same place sweet water and bitter?"*** The answer is "NO!" absolutely not; it is impossible for this to happen. Check your well. Listen to what you say. Is your well full of sweet water, or is it full of bitter water? What comes up in the bucket will tell you.

What is Wisdom?

Now, let us talk about "wisdom." How do you tell a wise man? Well, you remember the verse of Scripture that we shared earlier—***"A fool's voice is known by a multitude of words" (Ecclesiastes 5:2)***. Let us look at ***James 3:13*** from the Amplified Bible to understand the real principle of wisdom. It says:

> ***Who is there among you who is wise and intelligent? Then let him by his noble living show forth his (good) works with the (unobtrusive) humility (which is the proper attribute) of true wisdom.***

The King James states:

> ***Who is a wise man and endued with knowledge among you? Let him show out of a good conversation his works with meekness of wisdom.***

Before we continue, look at the definition of the words ***"fool"*** and ***"wise."*** The word ***"fool"*** means a person lacking in judgment or prudence. The word ***"wise"*** means having or exhibiting a capacity for discernment and the intelligent application of knowledge. With these defined parameters, look at what God says.

God challenges us with this question in ***James 3:13: "Who is there among you who is wise and intelligent?"*** Remember we are still dealing with the subject of the spoken word in this chapter in ***James.*** Here God emphasizes wisdom as being the character trait and sign of God's control of the life of the individual. Another way of saying it is that Jesus is Lord of that life. So, the person whose confession is controlled by Christ, according to Scripture, is wise and intelligent. Then He says to let that individual ***"...by his noble living show forth his (good works..."***

What are we talking about? What is the sign of a person's being noble? His conversation. Noble is not a word greatly used in the language today; however, its meaning is "one showing high moral qualities or ideals," or "characteristic of greatness of character." Another definition is "one having eminence or dignity." Now, God specifically states that kind of character is one who never speaks an unkind, critical word. He says in the verse that the truly committed Christian shows Christ's life in him through noble living. In this case, he does this by not being critical.

Then the Lord states he must ***"... show forth his (good) works with the (unobtrusive) humility (which is the proper attribute) of true wisdom."*** Here God says the Christian is to have an ***"unobtrusive humility."*** Unobtrusive is from the root word "obtrusive," which means "to thrust forward or push out, to offer or force oneself or one's opinions upon others without being asked or wanted." In other words, it refers to a person who tries to be in control and demands to be heard. It all has to do with spoken word.

God says we are to have an unobtrusive humility. This would be a holy quietness about our life submitted to Christ. From there, He is able to control us and speak His will through us. People who are strongly opinionated and speak their mind in every matter are, for the most part, not Spirit-led or Spirit-filled. When we are Spirit-led, Spirit-filled, we will have an unobtrusive humility: a holy quietness.

Then He states: ***"... (which is the proper attribute) of true wisdom."*** What is the sign of true wisdom? Just to keep your mouth shut and stay quiet. Never be critical - never be caustic - never be bitter - never be negatively adamant. Most of all, learn not to speak until spoken through. If you are about to say something and you are uneasy inside, do not say it. Always remember, when in doubt - DON'T.

Focus Questions

1. Read ***James Chapter 3*** several times. What are the key words and key phrases that are repeated in the text?

2. We see in ***James 3*** that the individual who can control his tongue can control his whole body. Are you in control of what you say? Commit ***James 4:29-32*** to memory. This is a good place to start to get your confession under control.

3. Is there something about your life that you do not like? Confess it in prayer, turn it over to God, and then praise Him that you are wonderfully made.

4. As stated in ***Proverbs***, ***"death and life are in the power of the tongue."*** Is it possible that those who are constantly critical of themselves release power for Satan to use against them? What are some of the faults in your own life that might be caused in this way?

5. As negative confession can tear down, positive confession builds up. Give some examples of positive confession in personal

relationships and from the Bible.

6. What are some of the specific sins that causes a person to become negative and critical?

7. What is negative confession a sign of in the life of the believer?

8. Can negative confession be an inherited generational problem or a form of bondage?

9. What is the definition for cursing? Why is cursing men and women the same as cursing God?

10. Why should a Christian not take spiritual instruction from a person who is negative or critical or uses foul or polluting language?

11. What is the fruit of the Christian? Is it another Christian won to faith or is it something else?

12. Look up ***Galatians 5:22.*** This is the character of Christ and should be the character that is increasing in the life of the Christian. Are these things increasing in your life?

13. Under what kind of circumstances does your confession reveal the state of your true walk with Christ in the inner man?

14. Memorize ***Proverbs 16:1***. Then let Jesus be Lord of your life, and ask Him to help you "speak only when spoken through."

15. Contrast the expression and nature of prideful and humble people? Define true humility as discussed in this chapter.

I’m Too Fat

I'm Too Fat

CHAPTER SIX

The Power of the Soul

There is a special aspect of ***James 3:6*** that I would like to consider in more detail. Looking into the later half of this verse, God makes a statement that reveals a major factor why the world is in its present condition. His statement is: ***"... and setting on fire the wheel of birth, the cycle of man's nature, being itself ignited by hell (Gehenna)."*** Now, what does that mean? It means that the world continues to "wax worse and worse" because of its ungodly confession. Men's hearts become more and more depraved as they speak negative words. Their speech sets power into motion.

Man Was Made Out of Mud

In the Genesis record, we find how God "spoke" everything into existence. All that we see and all that we are was spoken into being. God spoke into being the world, the stars, the air, the water, and the life that all make up the universe and the galaxies about us. God saw all of these in His mind and spoke them for one purpose: the benefit of His highest creation—mankind.

Now, God made man for one reason. He made him for Himself. He then gave man the choice of will. He did so in order that man, after the fall, could confess his sins and receive Christ as his personal Lord and Savior. This brought the glorious process of being born again by receiving Christ into his life. In this, whether it be Old Testament time (through sacrifice looking forward to Calvary) or New Testament, (looking back at the finished work of the Cross), God made a way through Christ for mankind to enter into the Kingdom of God. However, we must see here two things in this regard.

First, when it came time to make man, God did not "confess man." However, He formed man out of red clay, out of the earth that He had made for man. Then He blew the breath of life into His creature, and man became a living soul. When we study the chapters regarding this divine activity in Genesis, we find that God made Adam, the first man, for God.

He then gave Adam ***"dominion"*** (control or authority) over all the earth. What does that word mean? It means, in this case, the power to rule. God gave Adam sovereign authority as the master and lord of the earth. We must understand exactly how he ruled. He ruled by the spoken word. Adam's power and authority came by the spoken word. Sin, which is essentially rebellion against God's spoken word, had not yet come. Adam did not face rebellion from the creation, for all that was about him had been domesticated by God. Adam controlled and exercised dominion by his spoken word, which was an extension of God's spoken Word since Adam was not yet separated from God by sin.

Now, when Adam fell, he did not lose that power, but God pushed it inside him. Years ago, I remember a television commercial for a corporation that had a certain kind of rice. They spoke about the vitamins in that rice not being "shaved away." They gave a visual illustration showing the outer core of the grain being scraped or sanded to depict the loss of all nutrients. However, in encouraging you to buy their product, they said that the rice had been prepared in such a way that the vitamins were forced inside. It then showed two little pistons, one on each side of the rice, forcing the so-called health-giving substance inside. This is exactly what happened to Adam. That power of spoken word was bound into his soul.

Hocus Pocus

Men today are trying to take the power of the spoken word and generate it into something else. Satan has tried to cultivate it by the use of the "arts of witchcraft and sorcery." We know these commonly today as ESP, EST, mind-control, or psychic control. However, this power is really the nature of man bound to the inside: it is really soul power.

Perhaps one of the finest books ever written on the subject of this particular phenomenon is by a Chinese Christian, Watchman Nee. The title of the book is *The Latent Power of the Soul.* I urge every reader of this writing to get this book at your first opportunity. It will expose to you the spoken word and its power upon the lives and circumstances of people. Another book that will help you understand this vital subject is *War on the Saints* by Jesse Penn Lewis. Whatever you do, get the unabridged edition, which contains a detailed description of the whole position of Christians who are out of the will of God and into 'soul power' ***(II Corinthians 11:3-4; 13-15).***

Mind Over Matter

We are going to see more and more "psychic research" going on across the world, as men try to cultivate the mind into an instrument of control. Truly, the old idea of "mind over matter" is coming to pass. At one time, the Russian secret service (called the K.G.B.) trained people who have "psychic capabilities" to use these abilities in their service. However, they are dealing totally with the devil and witchcraft. To practice these things is to defy God's commandments in ***Deuteronomy 18***. Some information regarding those in the research program has escaped that country. Most who entered into the development of their mind and speech based on psychic power have lost their minds. When you deal with Satan, you get his reward.

God shows us in ***James 3:6*** that people who are critical of other people speak with a power. They are able, literally, to bind lives or circumstances by their spoken words. God says the world is actually being bound by the spoken word. Evil men speak evil things, and evil comes to pass as these words turn loose into the natural world the power of the demonic spirit world.

Even in America, people today are projecting themselves with their mental abilities into the realms of psychic activity they call phenomena. It is nothing in the world but demon activity. With the study of the soul and its power in the sciences of today, we see things such as hypnotism, psychometry, telekinesis and even the study of witchcraft becoming more prevalent in our society. Incidentally, this is an evident sign of the coming of the Lord.

As we move to the end period of history, there will be a revival of demon activity through the power of a man's soul. We are seeing telepathy today experimented with as a science. This is mind reading or projecting thoughts to another person's mind. As we stated earlier, the Russians have done a great deal of research in this area. They are trying to find out if one person's thinking power can dominate another individual in order to overcome them. It is truly the "battle of the minds."

In these activities, Americans today are playing with death. They are especially inviting Satan to take over their lives. Demons today are looking energetically for people who are playing with the psychic sciences. It is these who, like Simon the sorcerer in the Bible ***(Acts 8:9)***, without knowledge, will sell their souls for power.

Dear Christian friend, let me assure you that God never works through the soul power of the individual. In the end time, the man of sin (Antichrist) will operate through satanic power controlling him from within. The world will stand in wonder and awe at his ability, but his glory will be demon-controlled psychic force. The ultimate consequence of this experience is eternal banishment from God's plan and place. The tragedy is that all who follow Satan's program will burn with him in hell.

Straight Line Praying

Today, witchcraft has made its greatest moves in human history. People are excitedly delving into the darkness of the occult. They are doing this in response to its promises of power and extreme abilities for operating in the supernatural. They are really giving place to demons in their own lives. As we have already stated, God commands that we have nothing to do with these spirit forces. In ***Deuteronomy 18***, as well as in other passages, He declares that it is an abomination for a Christian to have anything to do with witchcraft or the occult. The unbroken soul of the individual cries for recognition. It wants to be noticed; it wants to be acknowledged and praised for its abilities.

We have said all of this about witchcraft to point out the power the soul has through confessed words. Even among Christians we find people today who use this power and deal with other people in a "straight line" in prayer. By that, I mean that they simply pray toward a person rather than in agreement with God's will for that person. The mind is like a radio transmitter. For example, have you ever been in a crowd and suddenly you turned to look directly into the eyes of a person looking at you? You did not have to look all around to find him or her. You stared directly at that person, and he or she stared back. Your brain is a power, and, in this instance, your brain and the brain of the other person were locked on each other like radar.

Prayer to the God in Our Room

I think one of the greatest statements I have ever read in this area is in Watchman Nee's book, *The Latent Power of the Soul.* Rather than try to explain the position of Mr. Nee, I am simply going to quote him verbatim.

> "The prayers in the Bible are intelligent and not silly. When the Lord Jesus teaches us to pray, His first words are: 'Our Father who art in heaven.' He teaches us to pray to our Father in heaven, but we Christians often pray to the God in our room. We should offer our prayer directly to the heavenly Father for Him to hear. God wants us to send our prayers to heaven by faith, regardless if our feeling be good or bad, or even if there be no feeling. If you pray to, and expect to be heard by, the God in your room, I am afraid you will receive many strange feelings and miraculous experiences and visions from the God in your room. Satan gives these to you, and whatever you receive from Satan belongs either to consciousness or subconsciousness.
>
> Someone may not pray to the God in his room. He may

direct his prayers instead towards the person for whom he prays. This too is most dangerous. Suppose you have a friend who is over 2,000 miles away from you. You pray for him, asking God, as the case might be, to either revive him in the Word or to save him. Instead of directing your prayers towards God, you concentrate on your thought, your expectation, and your wish and send them out to your friend as a force. Your prayer is like a bow which shoots your thought, desire and wish as arrows towards your friend. He will be so oppressed by this force that he will do exactly what you have asked for. You may think your prayer is answered. But let me tell you, it is not God who answers your prayer, for you have not prayed to Him. It is merely an answer to a prayer that you directed towards your friend.

Someone claims his prayer is answered because, says he, 'I have piled prayers on my friend.' Indeed, for you prayed towards him, not towards God. Your prayer is answered, but not by God. Even though you do not know hypnosis, what you have secretly done has fulfilled the law of hypnotism. You have released your psychic force to perform this act.

Why is this so? Because you have not prayed to the God in heaven; instead your prayers are projected towards, piled upon, and laid siege to, the person for whom you pray. In appearance, you are praying; but in actuality, you are oppressing that person with your psychic power. If you use your soul force in praying for a certain one - say you pray that he should be at least disciplined if not punished - the prayer of your soul force will dart out at him and he will accordingly be sick. This is a fixed principle of the soul. It is as sure as the fact that a person will be scorched if he thrusts his finger into fire.

For this reason, we should not pray a prayer that asks that a person be punished if he does not do what is expected of him. Such prayer will cause him to suffer, and thus make the one who prayed such a prayer the instigator of his woe. If we pray, we should pray to God and not towards man. I personally have experienced the ill-effect of such prayer. Several years ago, I was sick for over a year. This was due to the prayers of five or six persons being piled upon me. The more they prayed, the weaker I became. Finally, I discovered the cause. I began to resist such prayers, asking God to disengage me from what they had prayed for. And so I got well. In this connection, let me quote from a letter written by a believer (Mrs. Jessie Penn-Lewis, *Soul and Spirit*):

'I have just come through a terrible onslaught of the enemy. Hemorrhage, heart affliction, panting and exhaustion. My whole body is in a state of collapse. It suddenly burst upon me while at prayer to pray against all psychic power exercised upon me by (psychic) 'prayer.' By faith in the power of the Blood of Christ, I cut myself off from it, and the result was remarkable. Instantly my breathing became normal, the hemorrhage stopped, exhaustion vanished, all pain fled, and life came back into my body. I have been refreshed and invigorated ever since. God let me know in confirmation of this deliverance that my condition was the effect of a group of deceived souls who are in opposition to me, 'praying' about me! God had used me in the deliverance of two of them, but the rest are in an awful pit . . ."'[1]

Kill Your Will and Agree with God

Now, I realize that many people are wary of Mr. Nee and his teachings. However, I do urge you to consider this position. The facts he presents in his writing are profound truths that have to do with the binding force of the human soul. You can pray for an individual in a "straight line" (praying your will for the person rather than seeking and agreeing with God's will) and actually bring change. This, for want of a better phrase, is a demonstration of "the power of the human will." However, if you pray in agreement with what God's desire is for that person, they will not have a soul change, but a spirit change. Only through the spirit does God deal in saving the soul. You say: "How am I to pray then?" Always pray to the Father in the Name of Jesus Christ. This is God's way.

To be born again is to have the Holy Spirit draw us into conviction. From there, we make a choice of will for our lives toward Jesus by confessing our sins and inviting Christ into our hearts. It is not of ourselves, the Scripture says, but it is all of God. A gift from Him. There is no other way under heaven a person can be saved. When a preacher gives a high-pressure "invitation," a person - without deep conviction - makes a choice of will, but his salvation is false. America's best-known evangelist of the 20th Century says that 85 percent of all professing Christians do not possess God in their spirit. They have made a soulish commitment and missed God by the distance of Hell.

How many times in these many years as an itinerant evangelist have I been guilty of putting great pressure on people for a "decision" through what we know as the "invitation"? The purpose was, at any price, to get a man to declare Jesus Christ as Savior. In the process of this kind of a soulish endeavor, I dare say there are thousands of souls who profess to be Christians who have never genuinely met Jesus Christ in a born again experience.

We must let the Holy Spirit be free to do His work through us. The Holy Spirit must have complete control of our person. We must not incorporate any of our own abilities into God's power. If God wants to resurrect our abilities and use them by flowing Himself through them, then we must allow Him to do so. However, if God does not initiate and use a particular gift in your life, then, beloved, do not use it in an attempt to help Him.

The soul is a power. It is a force we have to reckon dead daily. We are to present it as a living sacrifice to God. It is only when we have reckoned ourselves dead to self and alive to Christ that the soul becomes a usable instrument in God's plan. Not what we do for Jesus, but what He does through us is true spiritual work.

How to Activate God's Power

God has given us in His Word the way to release His power into our sin-sick world. It is the power of praise and prayer from a heart that is broken before Him. As the world moves rapidly toward submitting to the power of the Antichrist, God is calling believers to resist the demonic onslaught and surrender their lips to be used by a holy God as instruments of praise, worship, and intercession.

I personally believe that, if people upon awakening in the morning would simply begin to praise the Lord all across the world, within a short period of time, revival would come. Then, if they continue in their praise to the Lord, Satan would be bound. ***"High praises"*** is God's plan to bring His presence. (See ***Psalm 149***) Then, His visitation upon us here will show the greatest miracle we can ever know. That is, for a time, men will so love Christ that their nature, their lifestyles, and yes, their conversation, will be "in Christ" continually.

What a joy it would be to be able to speak nothing but "life" to each other! It could come if we ***"humble ourselves"*** and then ***"pray" (II Chronicles 7:14)***. We must seek Him in brokenness and true worship. Again, if all men would praise Him in unison, His power would fall. Revival would come. Praise Him!!!

1 Nee, Watchman. The Latent Power of the Soul (New York: Christian Fellowship Publishers, 1972), pgs. 46-48.

Focus Questions

1. What does ***James 3:6*** tell us about the power of human confession for evil?

2. After God created the world, He gave Adam dominion (control or authority) over the earth. What happened to that dominion after the fall?

3. How does humanity exercise that dominion today?

4. Does this explain the battle that Satan wages to control the confession of those ***"made in the image of God."***

5. Does God ever work through human soul power? Who does work in this way? How does this process work?

6 Who will answer the prayers you pray to the "God in your room?" How do these answers come about?

7 What happens when we pray towards another person in a "straight line" rather than going to God? What kind of change does this bring about?

8. How is it different when we pray in agreement with God? What kind of change does this bring about and why is it important?

9. Have you ever experienced the effects of "straight line" praying in your own life or observed it in the lives of other? Discuss the impact and effects you observed in these situations.

10. What must happen before revival will come to the church of Jesus Christ?

11. The leading Evangelist of the 20th century has said that 85% of all professing Christians do not possess God in their spirit. They have made a soulish commitment and have never met Jesus Christ in a born again experience. What about you? Is the Holy Spirit living within you? Believing is not enough for eternal salvation. There is another step. The Scriptures are adamant about true salvation. God says: ***"For all have sinned and come short of the glory of God" (Romans 3:23).*** In this verse, we find that all are sinners; therefore, all must have a Savior. Then, the second step to salvation is to understand the consequences of our sin. ***"For the wages of sin is death; but the gift of God is eternal life through Jesus Christ our Lord" (Romans 6:23).*** Here God says that if we die in our sins we

will face (for eternity) separation in Hell. However, included in that verse is the statement that there is a gift extended to those who will receive Him. That gift is eternal life. Incidentally, a gift is something that cannot be earned. It must be received for free and not for labor. The great tragedy of eternity will be the millions of lost church members who cry out to God at the judgment that they were born again. They feel they have achieved new birth through their baptism, catechism, confirmation, or work and service by physical activity. The terrible truth of this is that they are lost—forever! Then, the third step, you must receive Him: ***"But as many as received Him, to them gave He power to become the sons of God. Even to them that believe on His name" (John 1:12).*** To be saved, you must open your life by believing in Him in faith. You must want Him with all your heart. Finally, we are told by John that He is standing at the door of every person's life, wanting to come in. He desires to save. He has made the way of redemption through His blood. He will save anyone who will repent: from the "guttermost" to the "uttermost"! You must make sure of this calling in your heart. ***"Behold, I stand at the door, and knock: if any man hear my voice, and open the door, I will come in to him, and will sup with him, and he with me (Revelation 3:20).*** Unless you are born again, you have no hope of controlling your confession. Just to make your salvation sure, let me urge you right now to pray this prayer from the depth of all you are—meaning every word:

> *"Father, in the name of Jesus, I believe in You with all of my heart; I believe You sent Christ for me. I believe He died for my sins. I am a sinner, oh, God; I have*

sinned. I come to You now in Jesus Christ's name confessing all that I have done. Forgive me of all of my sins. Thank you for your forgiveness. Lord Jesus Christ, come into my heart and save me. I receive you as Lord of my life. Thank You for saving my soul. And now fill me with Your Spirit. I claim my salvation and filling in Jesus Christ's name."

Upon accepting Christ as your Lord and Savior, seek out other Christians and get involved in a Bible believing church.

CHAPTER SEVEN

Caught in Satan's Trap

Now, let us look at how demons influence and control by spoken word. As we begin to share this part with you, I trust you will understand the message God has here. That is, words spoken from your mouth come from one of two sources - good or evil. Let us again look at the Scripture in this matter in ***James 3:14-18***.

It is imperative for you to understand that negative confession has its basic origin in demonic strongholds in the life of the individual. I believe these verses clearly bring this out. Once again, what is in the person comes out as we have read, ***"for out of the abundance of the heart the mouth speaketh."***

God establishes this origin of negative speaking in the ***14th verse: "But if you have bitter jealousy (envy) and contention (rivalry, selfish ambition) in your hearts..." (Amplified).*** Let us study for a moment what this means. Bitterness, of course, is the negative relationship of a person's personality to a past circumstance or to an experience with another individual. God says if you have bitterness in your heart, you are separated from God's life and flow. The Bible also states that, in this posture, you do not have answered prayer.

Jesus amplifies this in Matthew in the two verses following what we call *"The Lord's Prayer"* ***(Matthew 6:14-15, Amplified).*** Here He says if you do not forgive people who have trespassed against you in the area of reckless or willful sins, and if you have not given up resentment toward them, then your Father will not forgive you. In your unforgiveness, you cannot hear. Therefore, you must pull the roots of bitterness completely out by praise. The way to know all such strongholds in your life are gone is that you can talk about all those situations without becoming emotional. We have written more about this in our book titled *God Can Heal Your Mind.*

Now, if you have not praised God for every past experience in your heart and life, then according to the Word of God you will suffer two consequences. One, you separate yourself from God's will. Two, you do not walk in answered prayer. How do you know? Well, the Bible says that our "***... sins have hidden His face from [us]" (Isaiah 59:2).*** Those iniquities are known sins or strongholds that we have not submitted to God's removal. Another Scripture says: ***"If I regard iniquity in my heart, the Lord will not hear me" (Psalm 66:18).*** The word ***"regard"*** means to have sin in your life and to know it is there and not deal with it. So, coupling these verses with ***James 3:14,*** if you know you have in your heart contention and strife toward another person and do nothing about it, then you separate yourself from God.

Also, if you speak evil or something negative about that person, you do not speak by yourself, but you speak by a demon spirit. Now, before you turn me off, let us go on with these verses and see if God does not verify this. The Scripture states further: ***"... if you have bitterness or jealously..."*** What is jealousy? It occurs when your feeling of inferiority faces another person's circumstance or situation and passes judgment against it. This is because an inferior person feels defeated in the matter. So, now, you have two problems: (1) rejection in the life of the inferior person, and (2) separation from the will of God when it comes. Here Satan's wiles again bring spiritual defeat and separation from the voice of God within your inner man.

In our book *God Can Heal Your Mind*, we share from the Word of God that a person must accept himself. God made you as you are. He designed you before the world ever began. He even wrote out an order for what you would look like physically ***(Psalm 139:13-16)***. You have to accept the way God made you. This includes your abilities as well as yourself as you are. Then, you go from there, praising God for the fact that He did not make a mistake in your life. Until you do accept yourself the way God made you, you will never be set free.

So, to be jealous of another person is simply tantamount to feeling rejected in your own self. Satan's strongest weapon for defeating you is pride. It is the fuel that drives the internal engines of fear and insecurity. You really have nothing to fear or feel insecure about in yourself. "You are fearfully and wonderfully made!" God has made you, and you can have confidence from that posture in any circumstance.

God goes on to say in ***James 3:14,*** in the Amplified: ***"... if you have bitter jealousy (envy) and contention (rivalry, selfish ambition) in your hearts, do not pride yourself on it and thus be in defiance of and false to the Truth...."*** Now, envy arises out of rejection. Envy verbalizes its displeasure with another's position. It is one thing, however, to have envy within as a sin, but to verbalize it, to speak it aloud, further compounds the sin. Satan has set an even deeper trap to ensnare, hold and then consume the individual ***(Psalm 35:7)***. In fact, Satan has separated that person from God.

Let us go on from here in the verse. God then uses the word ***"contention."*** What does that mean? It means rivalry, opposition, selfish ambition, or contending and standing against. It means in your Christian walk you live as if you are in a contest. Again, dearly beloved, this is flesh in control of your Christian experience. In your carnal effort, you are doing your best to be better.

Caught in Satan's Trap

There is no place for rivalry in the life of a believer. According to His Word, God designs the born again person for one divine purpose: so that He can flow His mind and will through that individual. When you develop a rivalry with another person and his personality, you jerk your own purpose for being here out of the hands of God. You then begin to design your own life in an attempt to make it like that other individual's. What is worse, by your own effort, you try to be better than he is. How can you be better than another individual when you have never really become what God intended? Never forget that Satan's ministry is to divide - to separate the believer from God's will and plan and from other believers. Bitterness, or jealousy, or envy all separate us from God's will ***(Matthew 12:25-26)***.

You must become who you really are in Christ. Settle the issue that, when God made you, He did not make a mistake. He purposely designed you and performed in you His will for Himself. Until that time comes, you are never, ever going to be set free to become what you should be in Him. And furthermore, Satan will have won the victory in your life by defeating you and keeping you from becoming who you really are in Christ.

However, let us get back to the subject of negative confession. If rivalry with another person or selfish ambition drives you, and you contend by negative confession with the character of that individual, then you play into the devil's hand. Why? Because you speak by a spirit. You see, the Bible says, if you have these things "in your heart," Satan overwhelms and conquers you. Your joy is gone. You have no peace and, most tragic of all, you have no answered prayer.

King of Hearts

What does the word "heart" in this verse mean? It is your soulish personality. It is who you really are.

I once dealt by phone with a dear lady who was very jealous of a circumstance in her husband's life. She was so negative and contentious about it that she created a minor crisis in her home. When she called me for sympathy, I simply shared with her that the one thing God would have her do is keep her mouth shut. He wants her not to harangue, not to carry on, but to praise God for the circumstances involved.

After a while, she began to see this. Later in the evening, she called me back to share with me how this had so worked in her life that even her husband commented how he was grateful she was not upset about the matter. She called me in wonder to say, "It works; it works!" Praise God, I know it works, and she does, too. In fact, it is not "it" that works, it is HE working through us, His wonderful Holy Spirit, and He will work for you.

No matter what happens to you - praise the Lord for it. Never, under any circumstances, open your mouth to be contentious. Never speak in anger or be negative or caustic or critical or bitter in a circumstance. Why? If you do, first you separate yourself from Christ, and then you release yourself to Satan. You will allow him to create in you strongholds of bitterness, resentment and, most of all, fear. With fear comes insecurity and doubt about the person and truth of God. It destroys your faith. That does not mean you are lost, but it means you are not His. The flow of His life through your life has ceased. You are saved, but not in fellowship. You are no longer experiencing the glory of God's Holy Spirit. There is no resurrection power going through you ***(Philippians 3:10).***

Truth with a Capital "T"

On this same subject, God continues in ***James 3:14*** with ***"...do not pride yourselves on it and thus be in defiance of and false to the Truth."*** Now, notice that word ***"Truth"*** in the verse has a capital "T." Who is Truth? Jesus Christ. Who is the Way? Jesus Christ. Who is our Life? Jesus Christ. So the Scripture declares that people who are bitter, jealous, or contentious stand in defiance of the Truth. What does that mean? They are saying, "Jesus, you don't have a right to my life. Why, I can run this show better than you can; let me show you. I defy Your will for my life." Oh, how tragic! Their natures become adamant, and their attitudes become defensive in posture and critical in stand.

What does the Bible have to say about this? Well, they have separated themselves from God's flow through their lives. That is why I urge you to take no spiritual instruction from any individual who is negative toward another person. Why? Because he operates from hearsay. He is unable to give direct revelation to you. Why? The Bible teaches us the carnal Christian is literally "stopped up." God designed us to be a conduit of His glory. We are to be a channel of God's will. God's Spirit is to flow through our lives. All that each of us is to be is an unclogged branch, holding tight to the vine.

Phony Christians

You see now, there is not only the phrase, ***"defiance to the Truth,"*** but the rest of the verse says ***"and false."*** What is God saying here when He uses this word? He means "unreal." He means not in conformity with what is true. They are not "real" people. The common word for it today is "phony." Phonies are not real in Jesus Christ. He is not sovereign in their hearts. Their attitudes are not Christ's. They are not living in Him. They are not ***"...bearing about in their bodies the dying of the Lord Jesus..."*** They are not *"filled with the Spirit."* Jesus is not the *"Lord of their lives."* Christ is not their *"Life."* And so as they speak to you of spiritual things; they may even be saved, but they speak hearsay: only what they have heard others say. They give you the wisdom of their own minds. However, bitterness hinders their revelation. Contention and strife cloud their spirits. They have no revelation. How tragic is this kind of carnal life!

What are the characteristic signs of these people? They cannot receive constructive criticism about their own lives. They instantly defend themselves rather than receive it as truth. A person like this is filled with rejection and is separated from ***"Truth."***

While we are at this point, let me tell you about the individual who perhaps is never critical, but cannot receive criticism. You may have felt all the way through this book, "Well, I'm not critical, so he is not speaking about me." However, can you handle criticism? If someone gives you instruction, can you receive it?

Let us return to a verse I shared with you earlier. It is one of the great verses on rejection in the Bible. In ***Proverbs 15:32 (Amplified): "He who refuses and ignores instruction and correction despises himself, but he who heeds reproof gets understanding."*** Now, do you see the words, ***"He who refuses and ignores instruction..."***? In other words, no one can tell you what to do or constructively criticize you. If he does, you have an answer in your own defense for every situation. God says, ***"He who refuses and ignores instruction and correction despises himself."*** Do you know someone you cannot talk to under any circumstance? You cannot correct him without his becoming defensive and upset. He dislikes himself. He is filled with rejection.

"Rejection" is one of Satan's greatest doors into the human personality. From this flaw in our personalities we make our decisions, our judgments and decide our directions. Most of us draw constantly from that deep well in our personalities. It is filled with bitterness. We look at everything based on our own experiences, rather than from the filling of the Spirit of Christ. God says, ***"He who heeds reproof, gets understanding."*** In other words, "If you can handle reproof, you will be understood and received by others." If you cannot receive instruction in the right spirit without becoming defensive or upset, then it is evident you have separated yourself from God's plan for your life.

Let us continue our look at ***James 3:14.*** Here again God speaks of the individual who is ***"... filled with contention, or rivalry, or selfish ambition..."*** Remember, that ***James 3*** is built around confession. For the most part, everything in this chapter has to do with the spoken word. The purpose is to help you understand what happens to you when you are critical of another person. You are not only in defiance of God's will for your life; you are also false to the Christian life you are living. Please search this out in your own life. If you have taken offense with what I have said, then realize your offense is really with the Word of God. How tragic it is to be separated from God's will as expressed in His Word!

Forked Tongue

It is so important for you to come to the place where you continually submit your confession to Christ's control. If He can control your speech, then He can control your whole body. Your problem begins inside. It starts from the soul: within the area of the brain that is literally your reasoning self. It is who you really are. Beloved, remember the spoken word begins in the mind, for the speech is the slave of the mind. So, if you don't speak consistently and forthrightly, the Bible states that you are ***"...a double-minded man, unstable in his ways."*** Probably the best example of this is, if you say one thing to one person and then you meet another and say something entirely different to him on the same subject, God says you are double-minded. Or to use an old Indian phrase, you "speak with a forked tongue." That is saying one thing and meaning another.

Better still, you talk of the glories of God and the preciousness of Christ and the "resurrected life." You express to others the joys of salvation and victory in Jesus. Then you turn around the next moment and become critical of an individual. Now, this can be of you, a friend, or a non-friend. In any case, you should know that you have "spoken with a forked tongue" and that the Truth does not control your life. Jesus is not the Lord of your life; you are ***"false to the Truth."***

Not Many Teachers

At the outset of ***chapter 3***, the Holy Spirit interjected a verse of Scripture which is so relevant at this point. The first verse looks a little out of place until you really understand its true meaning. In the Amplified, the writer shares in ***James 3:1:***

> ***Not many (of you) should become teachers (self-constituted censors and reprovers of others), my brethren, for you know that we (teachers) will be judged by a higher standard and with greater severity (than other people). Thus we assume the greater accountability and the more condemnation.***

Now, I realize that we are dealing with this verse from a different perspective than is normally the case, but it really has to do more with the power of the spoken word than anything else. It points out that not many of us should become teachers. He advises us not to become teachers and ***"self-constituted censors and reprovers of others"*** because we are going to be judged by a higher standard and with greater severity than other people. Why? Because we design through our own minds what we feel are the truths and teachings of the Word of God. We then present them through spoken word. We teach other people our Christian principles. You say, "What is wrong with that?" If we speak on our own authority or based on what we have heard from others, rather that by God's revelation, we are in trouble. That is why He commands that not many of us be teachers. Why? Because Christ is going to hold us accountable for every word we speak from our mouths to the minds of other people.

Beloved, if you are separated from God, if you are negative in your attitude or spirit, you are out of the will of God. From this dark place, you are trying to tell other people about Jesus. They, in turn, are going to embrace your correction, direction, and reproof in the sense of your true attitude. In so doing, they are going to justify their own relationships to God by the attitude you have. If you are negative, you have set a course for them. Why? Because you are their teacher. God says you have assumed a greater accountability and more condemnation. God holds us accountable for what we say and what we do in teaching other people. Only babies in Christ condemn others. When you have babies teaching babies, there is no depth or life to impart. As the old chorus says, "Be careful little tongue what you say, and be careful little ears what you hear."

Caught in Satan's Trap

A greatly used evangelist of decades ago was walking down a street in a city where he was conducting a crusade. Now, this man had a tremendous ministry. Hundreds of thousands turned to Jesus Christ because of his firebrand style of preaching. One day a man staggered up to him on the street and, in his inebriated condition fell all over the man of God. When he did this, his voice, shaken by alcohol, declared to him, "You saved me in one of your revival meetings." Taken aback, the evangelist looked at him and replied, "It must have been me; it certainly wasn't God, because you wouldn't be in the condition you are now if it were He!" Our spoken word, arising out of hearsay, may make converts to ourselves or our way of thinking. However, only the word spoken by revelation will make converts to Christ. Beloved, our accountability is very great!

Trapped

Dear friend, may I share with you, never under any circumstances enter into a teaching position in a negative spirit. Never have anything in your heart that arises out of a spirit of criticism. Do not be upset with anyone; do not let the devil win the victory in your life and consume you and control your speech. "Why," you say, "Satan doesn't control my speech!" Are you critical? Are you bitter? Do you talk about other people in a negative way? What is your attitude? Are you always down? Do you curse? Do you criticize even yourself? You have no right to do this. And if you do it constantly without remorse in your own heart, then it is very evident that you speak by a spirit. The devil has trapped you. I urge you to read on so you will see this truth.

Where do you find that in the Word of God? Look at ***James 3:15***. Couple that verse with ***verse 14*** and you will see what kind of person you really are when you speak on the basis of bitterness, contention and rivalry in your heart. ***"Out of the abundance of the heart the mouth speaketh."*** Knowing and then telling another's fault is wrong. In fact, it is sin. It is none of your business.

If you are a Christian walking with God, when you see another person overtaken in a fault and in the wrong, you will pray for that individual or praise God for him. By doing so you will give him liberty and victory. However, you will not criticize him, nor will you speak negatively to another person about his conflict.

Band-Aid Believers

The Word of God states, in the ***15th verse (Amplified), "This (superficial) wisdom is not such as comes down from above."*** Now, what does that mean? Well, of course, the word "superficial" means something that bears no real depth. A superficial wound to the body is a minor abrasion to the outer dermis of the physical body, requiring, perhaps, only a band-aid. Better said, it is not really a critical, chronic situation. In this case, God uses the word ***"wisdom."*** God says that people who criticize other people in a negative way do not speak from revealed wisdom. Their total ability in the circumstance is their own demonically influenced mentality. It is superficial; it does not amount to anything in the Kingdom of God. When you hear a person criticize another individual, especially when the critic is not a part of the problem or a part of the solution, anything he says is spiritually ***"superficial."*** If you listen to the spiritual ***"wisdom"*** of that individual who is separated from God, you actually give mental assent and place to the devil.

That is a harsh interpretation of this passage from the Word. However, I believe this is justified because it says, ***"This (superficial) wisdom is not such as comes down from above."*** What does that mean? It means that it is not the mental heavenlies, or the abode of Christ in the speaker. It is not ***Philippians 2:5***, the mind of Christ Jesus. It is not ***Romans 12:2, "...but be ye transformed by the renewing of your mind."*** It is not ***Proverbs 16:3***, where we Christians trade our minds for His mind when we ***"roll our works"*** on Him.

In fact, when people are critical of other people, God specifically states that not only does that wisdom not come from Him, but also its origin is here in this world. Now, who controls this world and defines its ***"superficial wisdom"***? Who is the god of this world? Satan! This world is his home; it is not ours. This is the reason for an explosion in New Age thinking as Satan gets people to focus on mother earth as he prepares to bring them under a one-world government. Under Satan, mankind cares more and more about the environment here than about eternity there. As the songwriter has well said for the believer, "This world is not my home; I'm just a-passing through."

Now, if you are building your life here, then all that you have to show for your short period of life is here. It is evident that this book cannot minister to you. But if you realize on the inside that you are sick of soul and sick of spirit, you will discover that the vast majority of your problems are in the area of confession. For the Scripture goes on to say about criticism in ***verse 15 that it "is earthly, unspiritual (animal), even devilish (demoniacal)."***

Now, take a very close look at this. God says people who are critical of other people are "earthly." You say, we live on earth, this is "terra firma." What do you mean by "earthly"? In the Greek interlinear text, ***verse 15*** states: ***"This is not wisdom from above, coming down but (is) earthly..."*** Another word for ***earthly*** here is *"worldly."* The worldly or temporal or secular is opposed to heavenly, supernatural, spiritual things. This is Satan's kingdom.

God says people who are critical of other people are opposed to real spiritual things. You say, "I'm critical, and I'm not opposed to spiritual things." Let us be honest with each other. Have you felt opposition to what I have been teaching and to the Truth of the Word of God to this point? God is adamant regarding His position. A person can only be one way. In existence, or position, he is either one of two things, saved or lost. In salvation, he is either righteous or unrighteous. There are no two ways. There is no middle ground. Righteousness means "right-standing with God," not by our standard of righteousness, but by His standard. If you are critical you are worldly; you are not spiritual. There is no middle ground.

He goes on to say that people who are critical of other people by spoken word are also "unspiritual." Now, this word is self-explanatory. Not only are they in the world, but they act like the devil who controls the world. They do not act or react in the Spirit. In fact, they cannot do so when they are in that condition.

Poor Little Lambs

Then God uses the word ***"animal."*** He describes the person who is critical as an animal in his personality. The Biblical synonym for animal is carnal. Herein lies the root of all negative confession in the Christian's life - carnality ***(Romans 8:7)***. When you study the carnal church, which found its home in Corinth, you see Paul could not speak to them as to spiritual people, ***"... but as unto carnal, even as unto babes in Christ" (I Corinthians 3:1-3)***. A Christian who is negative toward another person in any form gives an evident sign that he is carnal or a baby.

A baby Christian rejects authority over him and will be ***"... as (a) sheep having no shepherd."*** He is an animal, a brute beast, in his conduct. Remember, lambs follow sheep; sheep follow the shepherd. There is the reason for so many conflicts in the local church. Lambs rebel against authority, especially God's delegated authority in the person of the under-shepherd (the pastor). When they do this they get lost in their rebellion. It is tragic when poor little lambs have lost their way ***(Matthew 9:36)***, particularly when God has given them an authority to lead them.

Now, let us look at the complete depth of this verse. At the end of it, God uses an incredible word ***"devilish (demoniacal)."*** It means that people who are critical of other people speak from an evil spirit. Over the years, I have watched the lives of people who are cynical and critical and have found their attitudes to be satanic. Pride is the very nature of Satan. People who feel themselves better than other people (even though they are always quick to deny it) are separated from God's flow, according to ***Philippians 2:3***. In fact, we ought to think of every individual as being better than we are. If we do this automatically, it is evident that Jesus is the Lord of our lives. To repeat, people who are critical and negative speak by a spirit. They are ***"devilish."*** Their speech is controlled by demons (demoniacal).

Never forget your words are power, for good or for evil ***(James 3:6)***. Satan sets up a situation, the person reacts in anger by speech, and the devil brings his consuming power into the matter. The devil is forever setting up ***"wiles."*** He engineers conflicts with other people. He constantly creates crises that bring bitterness into the heart, and in doing this, commits the individual to a direction of being negative. When he is allowed to create that climate in the personality, he conquers the Christian ***(Matthew 12:37).***

You must understand that God teaches at this point that our speech is either of God or of the devil. There is no other position. It is by the same standard that you are either saved or lost. You either have been born again or you have not. The evident sign that you love Him more than you love your own life is that you never speak critically about anything. Never let any spoken word pass your lips that does not bring glory to God.

Mark of Maturity

What you say is what you are. These two verses have so strongly emphasized, ***"... if you have bitter jealously, envy, contention, rivalry, selfish ambition in your hearts..."*** God commands you not to pride yourself on your negative confessions. Do not stubbornly think that you are right. If you are spiritual (filled and walking in the Holy Spirit), you will know immediately when you are wrong and will do something to correct the situation. In fact, because of deep conviction, you will, with all speed, break your spirit into submission to His Spirit. You will break your will. You will go to the individual who hurt you or harmed you (when he is aware of your attitude toward him) and say to him: "Please forgive me and my attitude." In so doing, you will break the stronghold of pride in your heart. Jesus will come forward in your person, and He will defeat Satan and his demons. Those who have the power within to straightway forgive those who have trespassed against them will walk in a flow-through victory. That is a cardinal mark of maturity.

Beloved, people who are critical of other people have no wisdom in the ways of God. All of their spiritual wisdom is superficial, according to the Bible. When you couple superficial wisdom with devilish attitudes and demoniacal declarations, you are not working in the Spirit, but acting like the devil. If, as a believer, you receive spiritual instruction from one of these who are thus separated, there will be enough error (flesh) sprinkled with truth to cause you to be directed in error ***(Luke 6:39, I John 2:11)***.

Caught in Satan's Trap

Focus Questions

1. What are some things that cause a person to speak negatively? Discuss how some of these factors have had an influence on you.

2 What is meant by the term "your heart" in ***James 3:14?*** Is this term often used in scripture with the same meaning?

3. What are some of the signs of a phony Christian? Are any of these signs apparent in your life?

4. Memorize ***Proverbs 15:32***. Do you "refuse and ignore instruction" or do you "heed reproof?" Can you see the outworking of the result of your response to correction?

5. Rejection is the greatest problem in the human make-up. It is from that posture in our personalities that the carnal person makes decisions, judgments, and directions. And it is from that posture in our personalities that most people are critical of others. How has this been true in your experience?

6. What does it mean to be doubleminded? Compare your answer to the definitions in a Greek (such as Vine's) and English dictionary. Do you show any signs of being double minded?

7. What does it mean to speak with a forked tongue? Have you ever experienced anyone who spoke that way? What was the result?

8. Conduct a self assessment by marking which traits most often apply to you. Are you...

critical or uplifting
bitter or joyful
negative or positive
down or up
curse or bless
complain or thankful

If you do the former most often the devil has trapped you. If the latter better describes your behavior, Christ controls your confession. Who controls your confession?

9. The Bible tells us that the devil is diligently at work setting up ***"wiles"*** to trap the believer in sin and compromise. One of his most common strategies is to create crises that bring bitterness into the heart and tempt the Christian to engage in negative confession. Satan wants to cause the child of God to surrender to bitter, critical and negative thoughts. Look up ***"wiles"*** in a Greek and English dictionary and compare with ***Ephesians 6:11***.

10. What ***"wiles"*** has Satan set up in your life? Have they succeeded?

11. Brother Bonner gave this exhortation: "never let any spoken word pass your lips that does not bring glory to God." How can we accomplish this?

CHAPTER EIGHT

Amused, Confused, and Bankrupt

In this final chapter of our study of ***James 3***, there are several more things we need to share with you. In ***verse 16***, God specifically shows us that negative confession is speaking by a demoniacal spirit. He then goes on to tell us that where we do have ***"envy, jealousy and contention, rivalry and selfish ambition in our hearts, there will also be confusion."***

Confusion is a person's inability to relate accurately to his circumstances. He is unable to comprehend. Webster's definition of the word is "the bringing about or the results of disaster." As an illustration, suppose an airliner is flying at 35,000 feet, fully loaded with passengers, and suddenly the pilot and co-pilot become very ill—so much so that they are unable to continue their duties in the flight. The only hope would be for someone in the passenger section to take over. However, there is no one who has past experience in flying. Finally, in desperation, the stewardess grabs the first person she finds and brings him forward. Whom has she selected? A farmer on his first flight, scared stiff. What does she do with him? She places him in the captain's seat and says, "Fly it." He looks at the dials, the pedals, the wheel, and the earphones. What one word could describe this petrified person? Confusion!

The specific synonyms from the Greek for the word ***"confusion"*** are unrest, disharmony, and rebellion. Now, in the beginning chapters of this book we shared with you the six things God hates. The last listed in ***Proverbs 6*** was: ***"He that sows discord among the brethren."*** God is adamant about the spoken word, especially that which brings confusion. He states, in essence, that where negative confession abounds in the life of the individual, there will be unrest, confusion, and disharmony.

In the light of this, look back once more to ***Proverbs 15***. Here again we see that a person who cannot take correction dislikes himself. The word for that is "rejection." By the same token, if you cannot submit yourself to the authority of another person, no matter who it might be under the circumstance, it is also evident that you have a problem with rejection.

The person who has not conquered his rejection by giving it over to Jesus will always face conflict or crisis by spoken word. He will find himself negative, critical, caustic, or bitter. He will look for the bad side of the other individual. He does this because he is trying to clothe or cover up his own inadequacy or his own inability. It is, in a sense, rebellion. And rebellion, as explained in the Old Testament is ***"as the sin of witchcraft."*** The rebellious person, according to that declaration, is controlled by satanic dominion in his life.

One final thing here is God's statement that He is not the ***"author of confusion."*** If God is not, then Satan is. The ***"destroyer"*** will do all he can to bring disorder.

Practice Makes Perfect

As we finish this verse, God states: ***"...and all sorts of evil and vile practices."*** Remember, in this chapter we are dealing with negative confession, criticism, caustic (sarcasm), and bitterness in the spoken word. What more can He say when He makes the statement: ***"... and all sorts of evil and vile practice"?*** The Bible teaches that people who are critical of other people have verbally involved themselves in evil. That is a terrible word. However, people who criticize other people are called what, by God? Evil!

There are two sources of relationship to life: God or the devil. God cannot be evil. Therefore, evil must have had its origin in man when he fell in the Garden. Remember, sweet water will not flow from a bitter well. In His statement here, God uses the term ***"all sorts."*** This describes the daily living level of the negative individual. He lives what he practices in life. Now "practice makes perfect," as the old adage says. He practices ***"all sorts"*** of evil and vile attitudes and actions. According to the Word of God, the individual who is constantly caustic, or critical, or bitter, projects himself into the negative, demonic world of evil.

Dear friend, what else can we say about this relationship? How adamant God is about criticism! How specific He is in His statement that people ***"... who can control their tongue can control their whole body."*** The individual who is critical, caustic or bitter is out of Christ's spiritual control for ministry and into His judgment upon their lives ***(Hebrews 12:5-8).***

God emphatically teaches that people who are critical of other people are separated from His will completely. He verifies this in ***verse 17***, where He defines ***"the wisdom that is from above."*** He declares that criticism is not from God, for that which is from God or ***"from above"*** is first of all ***"pure (undefiled)."*** That means it never finds anything wrong; it is never critical, never bitter, never puts anyone down. When it gets angry, it sins not; it bears no grudges; it is undefiled; it is healed.

The verse also says that wisdom ***"which is from above"*** (God revealing Himself and His will to man) ***"is also peace-loving."*** Who is the Prince of Peace? Christ! So, when Christ controls our hearts, what do we speak? We speak peace.

When He cleansed the Temple, Jesus overturned the tables of the moneychangers and said with absolute authority: ***"My house shall be called a house of prayer, but you have made it a den of thieves."*** Do you see what we are dealing with - ***"My house."*** Whose house? God's house.

In the same way, as Jesus makes His home in our hearts, He overthrows all in us that is contrary to His ordained purpose for us, then He fills us up with His peace. He overthrows the tables of our bitterness and rejection, and drives out the demonic moneychangers of critical and negative confession. Jesus was not part of the problem, but as we can see, He was the solution. When our peace comes from Him, ***"from above,"*** then the wisdom we speak will be peace. When Christ controls the believer's life, He lives His own peace-loving nature through him.

Going back to ***James 3:16***, He includes next the phrase ***"courteous (considerate, gentle)."*** What is that nature of Christ in and through the individual? Considerate, not inconsiderate. He is gentle. What does it mean? There is meekness. In ***Matthew chapters 5 through 7***, Jesus taught the Sermon on the Mount. In this teaching we received the Beatitudes. The word "beatitude" actually means this is what "our attitudes" should be. We should be like Whom? Jesus. When Jesus controls our lives, we are not critical, caustic or bitter, for that is not His nature. However, when He does not control our lives, then Satan takes over, and we become involved in the evil and vile practices which have their roots in negative confession.

The Flow-Through Life

By contrast, God says in ***verse 17*** that when we operate in revelation, or in His wisdom, or in His mind, we are "willing to yield" to reason. If someone has something to say to us, we listen. You see, the person who does not speak is on the other side; he is a listener. God help us to get out of the business of being speakers and into the business of being listeners ***(Ecclesiastics 5)***. The key is *K.Y.M.S. (Keep Your Mouth Shut)*.

One of the problems I had with my own children was that I was not able to minister "life" to them. The reason for this was that I was not a listener. In fact, I took the principles of God and began to enforce them on my children without listening to their personal needs. When they had a question, there was no answer except my own scriptural position based on my adamance and authority. One day, I woke up to the fact that I was losing my children because there was no gentleness in my attitude.

God commands the daddy to be tender with his children ***(Ephesians 6:4, Amplified)***. I believe the nature of Christ was gentleness. I believe it was in His eyes; it was in His voice; it was in His manner. It was certainly in His message and life. Even though God expects the daddy to exercise authority, at the same time He expects to find the gentle nature of Christ coming through him as well.

God states further in the verse that a Christian is to be ***"...full of compassion and good fruits..."*** Now, let us turn the verse around. The individual who is critical, caustic, bitter, or unkind in his confession is not compassionate, and does not produce good fruit. What is good fruit? That fruit, as stated earlier, is Jesus Christ extruding Himself through us. He can only do this when we yield ourselves to Him. What is the nature we have when we do that? Quietness, holiness, peace. In fact,

Galatians 5:22 says, ***"... love, joy, peace."*** We must never forget that when we get home to heaven someday, we are not going to be rewarded for what we have done in the Name of Jesus, but what He was able to do through us in His Name.

When you break down those words, you find the word ***"love"*** is "agape." This kind of love comes only from God. This is not man's ability to love, but is God's love to and through us. With it comes a joy that is "unspeakable." It is not some emotion we conjure up in the good times. It is becoming so like Jesus in our hearts that we have His joy. Peace! What kind of peace? That is Christ Himself, being Himself in us, in that we have ***"...peace that passeth all understanding."*** That peace is Jesus living through us.

God's position is that the person who is spiritual is full of compassion. When such a person sees something wrong with another person's life, he immediately becomes broken over the circumstance and begins to intercede. Instead of becoming negative, he becomes positive and broken over that individual's need. He becomes compassionate.

You see, the fruit of a Christian is Jesus Christ, and compassion is His nature. He wept over the lost; He wept over those who would not receive Him. He was broken in His heart over their lives. One of the evidences of Christ's life flowing through the believer is empathy. As we walk in Christ, we take on the needs and feelings of others. We share their hurts in brokenness. In doing so, we not only share Christ's life in ministry, we also share His intercession in praying for them.

Spiritually Tongue-tied

To conclude ***verse 17***, God describes the individual who walks in the spirit, who has the flow from above, as ***"... wholehearted and***

straightforward, impartial and unfeigned - free from doubts, wavering, and insincerity." What does all that mean? Simply put, this describes the nature of Christ through us. Without His nature living through us, we become—for the want of a better phrase–wishy–washy or double–minded. We are carnal and religious, or perhaps apathetic and dead. In that condition, we are never stable. We are always drifting with the winds of change. As a reed shaken by the wind, we blow in the direction of whatever we are experiencing at the moment. In this carnal state, if someone is critical, we listen. That is the evidence that we do not meet the description of ***verse 17***.

If we are out of the will of God, we will speak criticism by nature (the natural man). God says the person who has his lips under divine control, has given his confession to Christ. He speaks life. In fact, he can speak only the words of God and will not speak until spoken through. This is the evidence of being ***"wholehearted."*** Look at the root word "whole." Used here, it means completely controlled by Christ in his soul.

Next is the word ***"straightforward."*** If a person walks in the Spirit, you know his mind; you know his attitude; you know how he is going to act; you know the way he is. He is consistent and not counterfeit. How many of you reading this do not like the way you act? Or how many of you act one way in one situation and different in another? Straightforward means not to be double–minded or unstable in your ways. When you speak, speak only truth, and your speech will be straightforward. Again, another way to say it is, do not speak unless spoken through.

God says that the person who has his speech under Christ's control is ***"straightforward and impartial."*** What does He mean by impartial? The individual who has settled the spiritual issues in his own heart does not have partiality toward one person over another. He does not judge. He sees men as saved or lost.

You say, "Brother Bonner, you are creating an impossible situation. No one can keep from being judgmental. We all stumble and fall." Sad to say, this is right. However, God placed the standard here. We are speaking of evidences of the filling of the Spirit. If there is an inward desire to go on with God, the outward speech will show our growth ***(James 3:2)***.

What we say is what we truly are inside. Always remember, ***"out of the abundance of the heart the mouth speaketh."*** Satan knows this and will do all that he can to set up a scenario to get the believer to react rather than act. Remember that his type of confession is always negative. The devil's greatest tool of deception is negative, critical reaction produced by his wiles. It is into that place of bondage that he traps the believer.

Then we find the word ***"unfeigned."*** It means to be separated from all encumbrances. The individual who continually allows Christ to control his speech has it all together ***(James 3:2)***. What would be another way to say it? No matter what situation he is in, he is completely "content," or free. Ah! To be free! You can be. You say, "How?" By keeping your tongue under Spirit–control. Or even better, be "spiritually tongue–tied." Do not speak until you are spoken through. Do not give place to the devil. *K.Y.M.S., keep your mouth shut,* unless Christ opens it!

Are You Living a Lie?

Then He continues with the statement in ***verse 17: "free from doubts, wavering and insincerity."*** Does that not sound like what you would like to be? All this, again, is just the nature of Christ. If you will seek Him, His nature will consume you and change you. His quality will become your life: all by the binding of your words and choosing Christ as Lord. How can this be accomplished?

There are two steps toward being filled with the Spirit. One is confessing the negative side of your life in open confession, and then asking for and declaring your Spirit filling ***(Ephesians 5:18)***. The other is filling your soul with the living Word of God. This means being filled by studying and memorizing Scripture. In the process, you are filled with His Spirit.

We find this principle in ***Colossians 3:16***. Here is a way to enter into that position. You are to have your lips under complete control, never allow yourself to be negative. You are to praise God in all things. You are to begin your day praying, "God, in the name of Jesus Christ, don't let me speak until I am spoken through," or better still, "I agree with You for what is written in heaven for my life today" ***(Ephesians 2:10, Amplified)***. God says that, as the result of that experience, you will be free from doubts and wavering.

The opposite is for you to become double-minded. You will be speaking out of both sides of your mouth, depending on whom you are around at the time. This is being unstable in your ways. You will be filled with insincerity, and not with the Spirit.

What is insincerity? To be insincere is to be untruthful in your relationship with another person. If you live a Christian example before the church and then go out in the world and use filthy language, negative confession, and/or criticism of another's position you are insincere. You are unreal. You are living a lie. Your life is not truth. By today's terms, you are a fraud, a phony. In this case, you can check out your level of insincerity by listening to your confession. I like the statement in the King James Version, in the last line of ***James 3:17: "... without partiality and without hypocrisy."*** We do not use the word "hypocrite" much any more; however, the word still means to be two-faced. In this case, it means you are living a lie.

A Harvest of Righteousness

How wonderful ***verse 18*** is! In the King James Version, it says ***"And the fruit of righteousness is sown in peace of them that make peace."*** Therein lies the quality of a spiritually tongue-tied Christian. Look at it in the Amplified:

> ***"And the harvest of righteousness (of conformity to God's will in thought and deed) is (the fruit of the seed) sown in peace by those who work for and make peace - in themselves and in others, (that is,) that peace which means concord (agreement, harmony) between individuals, with undisturbedness, in a peaceful mind free from fears and agitating passions and moral conflicts."***

Here God begins with, ***"And the harvest of righteousness."*** Now, I love the word ***"harvest."*** This means the reaping of the field after it has come to the culmination of its growing time and its fruit has matured. Righteousness, again, means "right standing with God." The fruit of the righteous life of the individual is going to be the ***"harvest" (Proverbs 18:20).***

When you stand before God as a believer, according to ***II Corinthians 5:10,*** He will reward you for that which is good and that which is bad. As we shared before, He has already written down every word, every thought, every intent. You will be judged for these unless you have confessed them in this life and sought true repentance for them.

Yes, you can repent for words spoken, bad attitudes and satanic-dominated positions of your life. You can wipe out all of those negative things God has written down in Heaven for which you shall stand in judgment someday. Even the thoughts of your mind and the intents of your heart can be overcome by truc, rcpentant confession. A person can settle the issue here. He can go to that individual he has hurt or harmed and seek their forgiveness. If that is impossible, he can go to God, broken over the event and in a contrite heart seek forgiveness. God will forgive and wipe away the judgment with the Blood of Jesus. This form of confession overcomes and cancels out those sins recorded in heaven ***(I John 1:9)***. Then to top it all off, it releases the individual to walk in Christ, and His victorious life here.

For you see, we find the ***"harvest of righteousness"*** in the confession or the spoken word. Again I must reiterate that ***James 3*** deals primarily with the spoken word. Then, ***verse 18*** shows the results of positive confession, or words spoken through you by the Spirit of Christ. The Scripture teaches that the ***"harvest of righteousness"*** is ***"conformity to God's will in thought and deed."***

When God speaks through you words that He wants spoken, He brings with them attitudes He wants you to experience. In the process, the world, in seeing you, does not see you - it sees God. And the world, in hearing you, does not hear you - it hears God. The Truth, therefore, is being lived through you and you will find yourself never saying an unkind, critical, caustic, or bitter word about anyone.

When all your spoken words are in prayer or praise, then your attitude will be the projection of Christ. When the world encounters this position in your life, it will turn to Him. God then uses your words to implant His witness in the lives of "worldly" people. Through you

He sows seeds of eternal life. God then, through others, waters the soil. The final results are the increase promised in ***I Corinthians 2:8***.

How important is your speech! How important it is that you allow the Spirit to control it! How important it is that you hold nothing in your heart against another person! In fact, how important it is to *K.Y.M.S.!*

Then, going on in the verse, He says to us that in our speech, we will literally bring in a ***"...harvest of righteousness..."*** This means people, in hearing us, will be conformed to God's will in thought and deed. This, again, is speaking when spoken through. By His Spirit, God brings men to His will. In this profound statement lies the basis of all that we are.

Bringing in the Sheaves

In the light of this, let us look again at ***verse 18 (Amplified). "The fruit of the seed sown in peace by those who work for and make peace - in themselves and in others."*** The key phrase is ***"seed sown."*** With this thought in mind, consider again how what is inside of the individual is reproduced through spoken word. When there is bitterness inside, it expresses itself on the outside by bitter words. By contrast, when ***"a seed is sown in peace,"*** it produces peace, the person of Christ through the life.

Again, He states that ***"the fruit of the seed sown in peace by those who work for and make peace - in themselves and in others..."*** In the final analysis, what does it mean? Positive confession. Saying a positive word. Never being critical. Never being caustic. Never being bitter. Letting your "yea, be yea" and your "nay, be nay." Letting your conversation be in Christ, thereby producing the testimony of His will and purpose. Letting them hear Jesus in your speech. As stated earlier, the "seed is the Word of God." To sow it is to express its life to others by spoken word. However, remember the ***"sweet and bitter water"*** position.

People cannot receive spiritual truth from a negative person, who shows no harmony with God's Spirit. Therefore, they will reject it or forget it. It does not speak to their spirit. However, when Truth is ***"spoken in love,"*** it brings a harvest. Or, as the old hymn says, "We will come rejoicing, bringing in the sheaves."

Is Your Bucket Clean?

As stated earlier, what is in the well comes up in the bucket. Put another way is the Scripture we studied earlier, ***James 3:11: "Doth a fountain send forth at the same place sweet water and bitter?"*** The obvious answer is, "No." Sweet water from a bitter well still carries within its make-up the putrefying elements of death. Someone may have disguised the bitter water to make it taste sweet, but the problem still lies with the water in the well.

The water in a well reflects the taste of its habitation. If it is from soil that is iron-based, there will be a strong mineral taste from that environment. If the soil is sandy with a touch of limestone to act as a natural filter, the water is sweet and pleasant to drink. In this case, both will quench your thirst, but always the one that is purest has the better taste; it is sweet.

Therefore, rather than trying to treat the water by disguising it with a lying spirit, why not treat the soil? Why not, in this case, pray to be broken before the Lord ***(Isaiah 57:15, 66:2)***. Always remember the soil must be porous or broken for the water to form a well. When ground is hard and rocky, the water from a rain will simply run off, it will not filter into the soil. God says in ***Hosea 10:12: "Sow to yourselves in righteousness, reap in mercy; break up your fallow (hard) ground; for it is time to seek the Lord, till he comes and rains righteousness upon you."***

Farmers do not broadcast seed on ground without plowing it first. They crush and break up the soil to make it ready. Broken soil absorbs and holds the moisture. It then filters the water flowing through it and gives the taste of its own life to it. This union of soil and water will produce a well of water springing up from within ***(John 4:13).*** Oh, what joy to drink from the "Springs of Living Water," as the old Gospel song says.

By the way, what is the condition of your bucket? Is it rusty or clean? Was the bucket used to hold dirty mop water (criticism)? Or, has your bucket been cleansed and made pure by scalding fire and purging ***(Numbers 21:17, Isaiah 6)***? You might indeed have a well of sweet water, but if you keep dipping a dirty bucket into it the water will soon become bitter. If you allow others to continually dump bitterness and criticism into your bucket (your hearing) before long your well will become polluted. Then the water you draw from it will no longer be sweet and life-giving. The Bible teaches again ***"out of the abundance of the heart the mouth speaketh."*** Said another way, what you say is what you are. Protect what you are by keeping your bucket clean and pure.

Then, to finish ***James 3:18***, God declares ***"... (that is), that peace which means concord (agreement, harmony) between individuals with undisturbedness, in a peaceful mind free from fears and agitating passions and moral conflicts."*** Therein lies the healing and the signs of healing. People who are never critical, caustic or bitter speak the life of Christ, which is peace. That peace means accord (agreement, harmony) between individuals.

Remember, ***"Blessed are the peacemakers..."*** What do they do? They, through Christ, tie things together. They have learned that ***"a soft answer turneth away wrath."*** Cursed are those, literally, ***"...who sow discord among the brethren."*** The peacemakers speak by the Spirit of Christ.

Those who sow disharmony and distrust by negative confession on others or themselves speak by an evil spirit. Their practices are vile. Their biblical teachings are hearsay from other men rather than revelation from God. Their walk is not in Christ. Their well is polluted or dry. They thirst but are not quenched.

People who speak a positive confession, God says, not only ***"... sow harmony among other people that the fruit would be righteousness in their lives,"*** but they transmit to other lives that they have undisturbed and peaceful minds. They also are completely free from fears, agitating passions and moral conflicts. Why? Because in their lives they give thanks for everything. If someone criticizes them, they thank the Lord for it. It makes no difference to them. If they are agreeing with God daily for their lives, then they are walking in the Spirit. They are led of the Spirit, because they are filled with the Spirit. In this wondrous place, they are progressing daily in prayer that the Spirit might consume them and control them and minister through them. All these are evidences that Christ is in complete control of their lives. What a testimony!

We give evidence of all this through our spoken word. The person whose life is under Christ's control never speaks an unkind word. Would it not be wonderful if one could be of ***"...peaceful mind, free from fears and agitating passions and moral conflicts?"*** It can happen ***(Romans 12:1-2)***. However, you can only have it if your lips are under control and you yield your life to Christ fully ***(James 3:2)***.

The Devil's Trap

Remember the phrase "moral conflicts." Ordinarily, we use the word "moral" to explain sexual circumstances. However, Christians who have clashes in their hearts in a moral way are those who, by and large, are critical and negative.

Let me give you an illustration. Some years ago, a seminary professor was teaching a class about being careful in counseling situations. He shared how the devil could trap his students as he had trapped others who had fallen in their denomination. He stated that men should keep their lives clean so they would never be caught or cornered in a bad circumstance. Then, as he closed the class, he stated that the devil would like to destroy every person's ministry in that room by compromising them.

At the end of his class, he asked a very pertinent question of those in attendance: "How many of you here today feel that this could never happen to you, that you could never be trapped, or cornered or caught in a sexual situation that would destroy your calling?" There was a ripple of nervous laughter across the room as half of those young people raised their hands in assent to the fact that it would never happen to them. As he looked across his audience of those who would stand in future ministries and present the Gospel of Jesus Christ, the professor then wisely stated, "It will happen to you first. It is you who feel that it could never happen to you, in whom Satan will move the quickest."

God says in ***I Corinthians 10:12-13:***

Wherefore, let him that thinketh he standeth take heed lest he fall. There hath no temptation taken you but such as is common to man; but God is faithful, who will not suffer you to be tempted above that ye are able; but will with the temptation also make a way to escape, that ye might be able to bear it.

Satan can trap you, but he will have more resistance from the "quiet person" than he will have from any other. Why? Because the individual who is quiet has learned to listen. Let your lips be completely controlled by Christ. In so doing, you will truly operate in the ministry of "Bringing in the Sheaves."

Focus Questions

1. What are the causes of confusion in ***James 3:16***? What are the specific symptoms of confusion? How have these factors affected your life?

2. As we saw in the previous chapter, experiencing rejection has a devastating effect on the human personality. What sort of behavior results from rejection, if it has not been resolved in Christ.

3. How does rejection lead to the sin of witchcraft "in the hurting soul? What must the believer do to break the spirit of rejection?

4. What are the characteristics of a flow–through life? How is this accomplished? How does a Spirit–controlled person react when they see someone in difficulty or in sin?

5. Are you discouraged by the negative confession and its fruit you see in your own life as you have studied this book? What light does ***James 3:17*** shed on what you can do to be free from negative confession?

6. According to ***James 3:18*** in the Amplified Bible, how does positive confession lead to a harvest of righteousness? Have you ever experienced such a harvest? If so, describe it.

7. ***II Corinthians 5:10*** tells us that we will all appear before Christ at the judgement seat and "receive what is due" for the good and bad we have done. How can we cancel the effect of our negative words so that we can stand before Christ cleansed of these sins?

8. At this point, ask the Lord to reveal to you the issues of your heart and speech that need to be dealt with. Write out a prayer of confession to the Lord for the sins you have committed by spoken word.

9. List the people whom you have offended in what you have said or done to them, and ask the Lord to reveal to you how you should ask forgiveness or make things right with them in some way.

10. What does it mean to be a peacemaker? What is the effect of a peacemaker's life? How is this accomplished?

11. Have you ever played the role of peacemaker or experienced someone fulfilling this role in a church business, or other group with which you have been associated? Discuss the situation and the peacemaker's involvement in bringing about resolution.

CHAPTER NINE

The Good Life

As we move toward the close of this writing, there is yet one area we must cover. In it we find explicit instructions for Christians regarding the spoken word. It also brings to light the Biblical position of our relationship with others who speak negative words. What are we to do? How are we to act? And how are we to handle the circumstances involved? God has a plan, and He has detailed it for us in ***I Peter 3:8-12 (Amplified):***

> ***Finally, all (of you) should be of one and the same mind (united in spirit), sympathizing (with one another), loving (each the others) as brethren (of one household), compassionate and courteous—tenderhearted and humble–minded.***
>
> ***Never return evil for evil or insult for insult—scolding, tongue—lashing, berating; but on the contrary blessing—praying for their welfare, happiness and protection, and truly pitying and loving them. For know that to this you have been called, that you may yourselves inherit a blessing (from God)—obtain a blessing as heirs, bringing welfare and happiness and protection.***
>
> ***For let him who wants to enjoy life and see good days (good whether apparent or not), keep his tongue free from evil, and his lips from guile (treachery, deceit).***

Let him turn away from wickedness and shun it; and let him do right. Let him search for peace—harmony, undisturbedness from fears, agitating passions and moral conflicts—and seek it eagerly. Do not merely desire peaceful relations (with God, with your fellowmen, and with yourself), but pursue, go after them!

For the eyes of the Lord are upon the righteous—those who are upright and in right standing with God—and His ears are attentive to their prayer. But the face of the Lord is against those who practice evil—to oppose them, to frustrate and defeat them.

The Mark of Maturity

Let us look at these verses in the light of God's declared position for the Christian's spoken word. God begins by destroying all reason for being negative about another individual. He makes this statement to His Body, the Church, telling us to be of the same mind. You must understand the doctrinal relationship expressed in this declaration. The Scripture teaches, ***"How can two walk together except they agree?"*** Again, God says that we are to be of the same mind. In another place, He shares that we are to be ***"... one in the Spirit."*** In the body ministry there must be unity of faith.

Satan always moves to separate the church by setting up divisive circumstances within the body itself. This prevailed in the Corinthian church as expressed in ***I Corinthians 3***. Here Paul reproves those who had forsaken God's control over their lives. They had envy, division and strife and walked as men in the flesh. God commands the Christian not to walk in the flesh, but to walk in the Spirit. To walk in the Spirit means you can hold nothing in your heart against another individual. To walk in the flesh or to walk as a man is to be negative, critical, caustic and/or bitter. In fact, ***Galatians 6:1*** gives us the real mark of spiritual maturity in the believer's life. God says:

> ***"Brethren, if a man be overtaken in a fault, ye which are spiritual restore such a one in the spirit of meekness, considering thyself, lest thou be corrupted."***

Paul wrote the book of Galatians to the churches in Galatia under the inspiration of the Holy Spirit. His purpose was to reach them in time to stop their backsliding. They had turned to the legalism and the judgmental spirit of teachers from Judea. Satan had so moved in them that they had even gone back to the practice of witchcraft and the worship of demons. This is happening in the church of today as it blends with New Age teachings that negate the person of Jesus Christ. Men have compromised their walk of faith by trading if for the works of religion. Satan is the author of religion. His works of confusion have established over 20,000 denominations in America alone.

Paul, in dealing with the Galatian Christians, reminded them that there is only one Gospel and shared with them how to receive it. He then related how, by God's leadership, he went and communicated the Gospel among the Gentiles. He continued by telling them how to be right with God and emphasizing that Jesus Christ is the total source of everything. Finally, he spoke of our inheritance in Christ Jesus and planted the Galatians firmly on Jesus Christ as their liberty and strength. Through Him, the power of the Blood breaks the bondage of Satan, his demons, and his bondage in and through us if we be crucified with Christ.

When we are established in Christ, He begins the ministry of the

Holy Spirit through us. We are no longer critical and negative which, in the past, brought us, as well as the one who heard us, into more bondage. We see others through the eyes of Christ. This is what Paul was saying in ***Galatians 6:1***. If we see someone overtaken in a fault, then we will seek to restore that person back to relationship with God and with His Body. We will do it in meekness. This means they have no sense of superiority; only humility motivates us.

Christ calls a person who is filled and controlled by the Holy Spirit a peacemaker, or one who restores. Spirit-filled individuals do this restoring, all the while watching within themselves lest they be tempted. Pride says, "That could never happen to me." Brokenness says, ***"There but for the grace of God go I."***

Beloved, I beg you never to say, "It could never happen to me," for what you sow you will also reap. I have witnessed this many times in my 40 years of ministry. Stay humble, stay broken, and whatever you do, *K.Y.M.S.* When you see someone in fault, learn to restore him. It is the evidence of your maturing in Christ.

United We Stand

Returning to ***I Peter 3***, consider ***verse 8*** in which God commands us to ***"be of one and the same mind (united in the Spirit)."*** When we have been broken before the Lord, we become a part of each other's lives or "body." This is called renewal, or being one in the Spirit ***(Philippians 1:27)***. An illustration from another area of the Scripture teaches us that if the physical body has one part that is diseased, the rest of that body attends to that one area until it is healed. The reason is that when one part of the body hurts, the whole body suffers.

Here is the way to identify a local church that is committed to ministering according to God's plan for it. If the body (or members) are healed spiritually, they will walk together in agreement ***(Amos 3:3)***. They will submit fully to the Lord. In this process, the Spirit of God prevails over that church's atmosphere. If the body is diseased in one area and the whole church moves to minister to that diseased area, that church is a truly spiritual body. However, if there is contention within the body and the body does not move to bring healing to itself, but separates, then you know that the church is "sick or dead."

As a case in point, cancer attacks healthy, living cells and destroys them. Bitterness is a cancer to the soul. When the cancer of envy, division, and strife enters into the church body, it will cause the church to die. Just as in human death, the first thing that leaves the body is its spirit. The second thing to occur is decay. The only thing that keeps the dead body from dissipating is embalming. Such is the condition of many churches today. The Spirit has gone, and it is dead. However, we still attend the funeral every Sunday. Negative confession killed the body (church). There is no life, no moving of the Spirit. The members have embalmed the church with religious activity. Since the physician could not heal himself, his medicine was not true.

The world has yet to see a church so totally committed to Christ that it operates as a body fully united in the Holy Spirit. If that kind of church existed, its outreach would be so formidable that Satan would make every move he possibly could to destroy it. Yet the greatest area for deception as far as the kingdom of Satan is concerned is the local church of today. He, for the most part, rules it. In fact, he has to. The danger the devil faces is that if just two people agree to pray the will of God, he is powerless and defeated. What would happen if a whole church prayed in unison? ***(Matthew 18:18-19)***

I am not against the local church. In fact, I believe that if a person is truly saved he will be involved in the church. He will be under pastoral authority, submitting and serving in the community. God commands it, and the evidence of being filled with the Holy Spirit is that we will be obedient. One of the best ways to tell if you are walking in the Spirit is that God has placed you in a local church body, in which you are serving with evidences of His will working through your life. If you are not serving in a local church body, then you have deep agony of soul, because you are out of the will of God ***(Hebrews 12:5-12)***. God will chasten the true believer who is not attending and ministering through Christ's local church. He commands us in ***Hebrews 10:25:***

> ***Not forsaking the assembling of ourselves together, as the manner of some is but exhorting one another; and so much the more, as ye see the day approaching.***

Joy as Part of the Family

As we have stated time and again in this book, the action that destroys the "life" of the church today is negative confession. However, in these verses in ***I Peter***, God shows us how to remedy this and defeat Satan at his strongest point. In fact, God demands that we do so. In ***I Peter 3:8 (Amplified)***, He declares that we should be ***"... united in the spirit,"*** and then that we are to ***"... sympathize with one another."*** Here, He tells us to bear one another's burdens by sharing another's personal conflict. To be in sympathy with is to have joined the circumstance and become prayerfully involved in the problem. This is the result of becoming one in the Spirit. You become a part of God's family. You are brothers and sisters in Christ. This is the command of God. The fact is that when you truly walk in the Spirit and God's power and plan is operating in your life, God says you will sympathize with one another. Failure to do so is direct evidence you are not filled with the Spirit.

He goes on to demonstrate this position in the rest of the verse, where He says ***"loving (each the others) as brethren (of one household)."*** I have fond memories of family reunions. Two very rewarding times in my life as a child were Thanksgiving and Christmas. It was then that we drove back to a little town in South Central Texas called Cuero. There were eight children in my mother's family. Many of those children had children. When we all converged upon an uncle's farmhouse, there were great numbers of kids. I remember the front porch on that old house where all the men would sit and talk. I can recall going into the house where on the wood stove would be the things prepared for the meal, such as turkey and dressing. The sights, sounds and smells were beyond words!

I even have fond remembrances of having to wait until the adults were through eating, and of sitting at the second table with the rest of the children. For you who are not aware of what that is, back in those days, the adults ate first. Then, when they had finished, they allowed the children to come to the table and eat their meal. There were always great fears of the best parts of the turkey being gone. However, because that was "turkey country," there always seemed to be enough for everyone there, as well as some remaining for snacks all afternoon. My mother's family was very close at that time and still is now. However, one of my fondest memories is that there was always laughter when they got together. It was truly family!

Mi Casa, Su Casa

Now, let us look at the church, or better still, the family of God known as the ***"body of Christ."*** God states that we are to ***"... love one another***

as brethren of one household." The local church is His outreach to the community. God commands you to be a part of a local body in service. The Scriptures teach the child of God to assemble with other Christians. You find this in ***Ephesians 4:11-14.*** God has called His pastor as an overseer of the flock (family). He is the under-shepherd over the local church body ***(I Peter 5:1-5)***. The Spirit–filled, walking–in–Christ Jesus Christian will be led by the Holy Spirit to become a part of such a body.

The point is this. You can tell in what relationship you walk with Christ based on your love and activity in the local church. You have a specific gift by which the Holy Spirit ministers within the body of believers. These are listed in ***Romans 12.*** God gave you that gift at the moment of your salvation for one reason: to operate within the local New Testament Church. God's commandment is ***"Not forsaking the assembling of ourselves together..."*** This means we are to come together as a body, so that the Holy Spirit can work through us as a united body of believers. In the process, God ministers to the needs within the body, Christian to Christian first. Then, through the body itself, Jesus Christ extends his life as an outreach to the entire community.

God desires that we be a part of and serve through the local church. Every believer has at least one gift of ministry out of the seven gifts of ***Romans 12***. A gift is Jesus Christ performing His ministry through the Christian. All seven of these gifts make up His life and ministry to the body. Bible study and prayer perfect a spiritual gift. As the Child of God grows in grace and knowledge, the particular gift begins to surface in his relationships with people. This is how the gift develops. Always remember, a gift is Jesus Christ being Himself through you. Do you know your gift? Study ***Romans 12.***

Beloved, you can tell at what level you walk with Christ based on the love and desire you have to function within the local church structure itself. If you walk in Him, you will build your entire life around being part of God's Family. You say, "Why?" Because those members within your local church are going to be closer to you than your own family. They will become your family—your mothers, fathers, sisters and brothers. As the Holy Spirit joins you to the church in which He would serve through you, you will become dependent upon the spiritual gifts of others who walk in the same realm of faith. You will need them, and they will need you. This is the way the body functions. This is the way that God has made it. He, through you, ministers to others with needs, that there might be healing and oneness with Christ Jesus.

You will find as you grow in Christ that you no longer possess your possessions. You will have transferred ownership of all to Christ. It is at that point you begin to live for others in your life. In Him, you are given to hospitality ***(Romans 12:13)***. Your home will become open to your church family. It will be "My house is your house," or in Spanish, "Mi Casa, Su Casa."

So, as God deals with us in ***I Peter 3:8***, He talks about the body and how we are to react to it. We are never to be negative, critical, caustic or bitter about anyone, especially those in our own family. According to God's Word, no Christian has the right to speak a critical word about another. God commands us also never to speak a negative word about the pastor, God's called man. The Scripture literally teaches ***"... touch not mine anointed..."***

I have often felt that "touching the anointed of God" by spoken word is a good test to see if a person has been born again. If he comes under retribution for the negative confession, then you know that he has met God in a born again experience. However, if God does not deal with him by His ministry of chastisement or scourging, then it is evident that he is not a Christian. If you would like to know more about this doctrine, I urge you to study ***Hebrews chapter 12***. Also, we have published a book titled *Brokenness, The Forgotten Factor of Prayer* that explains these principles.

So, God declares to Christians that He expects them to be ***"united in Spirit, sympathizing with one another, loving (each the others) as brethren (of one household), compassionate and courteous, tender hearted and humble."*** This means we are to deal with each other in a compassionate and courteous relationship. A Christian has no right to be negative, and those who are, find themselves separated from God's will. In fact, according to the Bible, they are sick. This does not mean they are sick in their physical being. However, this bitterness will ultimately bring them to such sickness, for the Word says , ***"bitterness dries up the bones."*** They are sick in their spirit, as we will see from the next verse.

In view of this, God commands us to be compassionate and courteous. If we see some tragedy in the life of another person, how are we to handle it? Very simply, by prayer or praise! We are not to speak to others about it. We are not to be critical, or caustic, or binding in the area. God commands us to be ***"tender hearted and humble."*** Christians are the only ones who take their wounded and bury them alive. Why? Because it is a trait of Satan to move in the life of a negative Christian and cause him to be critical of a person who has fallen into sin. God commands us to pray. The devil's way is to gossip in order to destroy both persons involved—the one spoken about and the one speaking. The Spirit–filled Christian on the other hand should *K.Y.M.S.*

One Hundred Years From Now

What is our reaction to be to the conflict in another person's life? We are to be ***"tender hearted," to be "humble."*** That means we are to be quiet in our spirits and loving in our hearts. You can definitely know the level of your walk with Christ based on the confession you have about other people. You know who and where you are in your walk. How? Jesus states, ***"...out of the abundance of the heart, the mouth speaketh."*** So, if you are critical, caustic, bitter, negative, or unkind in your confession or conversation, then you are diametrically opposed to God's plan for your life's fullness. The evident sign of being filled with the Spirit and walking in Christ is that we are acting as brethren, one to another. We are to be of the same "households" and we are to be ***"... compassionate and courteous, tender-hearted and humble."*** Another way to say it is, ***"Blessed are the meek, Blessed are the pure in heart."*** Or to paraphrase, "Blessed of God are those who are committed to God and do not speak unless spoken through."

Let us look at ***I Peter 3:9*** and see the power negative confession has on the life of the Christian. I know of no other passage in the Word of God that brings so strong a case against criticism. In fact, through this, God shares with us that people who are critical of other people have desperate needs. Let us look at the verse in the Amplified:

> ***Never return evil for evil or insult for insult—scolding, tongue–lashing, berating: but on the contrary, blessing—praying for their welfare, happiness and protection, and truly pitying and loving them. For know that to this you have been called, that you may yourselves inherit a blessing (from God)—obtain a blessing as heirs, bringing welfare and happiness and protection.***

Here God emphatically states that if someone criticizes us we are not to return the criticism. That is regardless of that person's life or character or our right to defend ourselves. In fact, this is a measure of maturity. It shows the spiritual quality of the life of the Christian. When an individual criticizes a Christian, he must receive it with praise. He must thank God for it.

You see, dear friend, He commands us not to return ***"... evil for evil, or insult for insult."*** It would be so easy to respond to the offense against our own person by becoming defensive. In other words, if someone were critical of you, it would be very simple to turn it around and speak negative in return. However, this Scripture makes very evident that God commands us not to do so. If we return negative for negative, we show that we have taken offense in our person. This is the true evidence of pride in our lives.

Several years ago, through a friend, I heard of an evangelist who had made a statement regarding my character. This bothered me for awhile until, finally, I took my wife several hundred miles to the place where this man lived and sat down with him and his pastor. I spoke of the circumstance, getting ready to defend myself. When we confronted the man with what I had heard that he had said, he denied having said it. This brought into suspicion the statement of our friend who originally shared with us what the evangelist had said. I suddenly discovered that one of these men was not telling the truth. Either my very close friend had made up this preposterous tale, or the man I was now facing was lying.

Did I become incensed? It would have been easy to do so; however, I had been preaching the message of praising God in all things for a number of years. As I sat there, God nudged my spirit and said, "Now, can you take it? Can you take criticism, even though it is false, and stand with it, or are you going to have to defend yourself?" I apologized for even having brought up the subject. I also sought forgiveness for having put the pastor on the spot, as well as this member and evangelist of his church. We excused ourselves and left.

God never hurries, but He is never late. Time is on the side of the Lord. If a man loves God and is committed to Him fully, his character will be defended by his life and by the flow of God through his spirit. We do not have to defend ourselves under any circumstances. God says so here when he states, ***"Never return evil for evil or insult for insult..."*** As my dad used to say, "You will never know the difference one hundred years from now anyway."

Going deeper into the verse, God then states: ***"... scolding, tongue–lashing, berating..."*** In other words, if someone raises his voice, you are not to take recourse in the matter, but only to stand in praise. Now, I recognize there are perhaps some people reading this who disagree totally with this perspective on the Word of God. All I ask you to do is read what this verse says.

God teaches, ***"Blessed are the meek."*** Now, that word ***"meek"*** does not mean one who is weak and cowers down under the table at the first sign of conflict. The word ***"meek"*** means one is so full of Christ that he (or she) is mild, patient, and long-suffering. The meek are never caustic or bitter. The meek individual is one who is so filled with the Spirit of Christ that, even in the midst of crisis, there is praise. Jesus is all that matters. Also, the meek individual has learned by experience to take the source of his conflict to prayer and praise. He does so by praying for the person who has despitefully used him and persecuted him ***(Matthew 5:5)***. Then he enters into a posture of praise for God so dealing in his life.

Another way to phrase this is ***"turning the other cheek"*** or ***"giving the cloak."*** However we say it, God commands us not to return ***"... scolding, tongue–lashing..."*** And then He says, ***"berating."*** This is an unusual word, but it simply means to angrily scold or put down. If someone puts you down, do you have a tendency to retaliate from your own violent feelings? This is a check to see where you walk spiritually with God. ***"All things work together for good,"*** and one of the greatest character building circumstances in the life of the Christian is crisis. When a person enters into crisis, particularly one based on personal criticism, there develops within that Christian oneness with the life of Christ ***(James 1:23).***

Call the Cops

Further in this verse, God states: ***"... but on the contrary blessing—praying for their welfare, happiness, and protection."*** Let us begin by looking at the word ***"contrary."*** To best illustrate it, suppose an individual says he is walking in the Spirit. He testifies that Jesus Christ is the sovereign Lord of his life. However, due to a circumstance (wiles) set up by Satan, he becomes negative and critical, caustic, or bitter about another individual who has been negative toward him. This is contrary to God's plan and purpose for his life.

"Contrary" simply means opposite in position, or mutually opposed. Another way to state it is that a contrary person is temperamentally unwilling to accept control or advice. Now, that is the true character of the critical individual as described by God. What comes out of your mouth under pressure is what you really are. The word ***"contrary,"*** in this case, means the believer is to act in exactly the opposite way to the one who is insulting him or subjecting him to evil. Such a person is acting out of a ***"contrary"*** relationship to God. He acts contrary to what God demands of him. In this case, however, God states when one scolds or berates a believer, instead of responding in anger, the believer is to bless the person by praying for him. It is the epitome of growing in Christ. Never react—act. You lose your victory by your reaction. In this case, by your negative confession ***(Matthew 15:11).***

The book of ***I Peter*** is a declared witness to people who want to go on with God. By "going on", I mean wanting to be in total commitment to the Lord Jesus Christ and walking in His fullness. However, as we saw in ***chapter 3***, the Christian who is negative, critical, caustic or bitter stops the work of God in his own life and the flow of God through his life. I realize this is hard—but, again, the person who can control his lips can control his whole body.

The object of our entire faith walk is for God to transform us into Christ's life. The Holy Spirit within us begins to change us from the inside out. He conforms us to Christ's Image. With conformation comes His life through us as we grow in Him. We take on not only His character, but His characteristics and life-style. In light of this, ***James 2:23*** in the Amplified gives us a complete picture of His nature and life as He seeks to live it through us. It states:

> ***When He was reviled and insulted, He did not revile or offer insult in return; (when) He was abused and suffered, He made no threats (of vengeance); but He trusted (Himself and everything) to Him who judges fairly.***

Herein, God describes the life and personality of Christ. If you are born again, He lives within your being. When you abandon your life to Him, He takes over and His nature becomes yours. With the takeover comes His attitude and attributes. Your nature will change to His. Your reactions will become actions of praise in the midst of all tribulation. What comes out of your mouth in a crisis shows the level of your maturity in Christ.

What a great tragedy it is when a group of Christians speak negatively about one another. God says this is wrong. God commands them to pray and to agree with Him for that person's life. Again, the Scripture teaches, *"... but on the contrary, blessing—praying for their welfare, happiness and protection..."*

SPIRITUALLY BANKRUPT

Let us consider this verse in its true perspective. What it is saying to us is this: If we see an individual criticizing another person, God commands us to begin immediately praying for the one criticizing. Why? Because the individual who is critical of another person is speaking by an evil spirit. We shared this with you out of the third ***chapter of James***. Our proper position is to immediately contend in prayer for the person speaking. We are to go to God and believe God for his life. Through prayer, we are to bind Satan in the person's speaking. As we pray, we are to reckon that Satan cannot defeat that person's life or character by causing him to criticize.

According to God's Word, the person who is unkind in words needs ***"welfare."*** That is not in the ordinary sense of the word used today for government income for the poor. The person who is assassinating the character of another individual is saying to you: "Deep inside, I'm troubled - I'm disturbed - I am not right - I have problems - and I need help. I am separated from God." This is what the Bible is declaring to us - that we are to pray for the spiritual welfare of the negative individual.

People who speak critically speak from a troubled heart. They have desperate needs, as has been pointed out in past chapters. God lays it on the line here when He states that these people are in need of ***"welfare."*** In essence, they are spiritually bankrupt.

In addition, they need ***"happiness."*** Now, that is self–explanatory. God says that people who are critical of other people are those who desperately need happiness.

The fruit of the Spirit are listed in ***Galatians 5:22-24.*** Within this group is the word ***"joy."*** Now, remember that this fruit is the nature or person of Christ living through the life of the Christian. The Holy Spirit is within us to conform us to the image of Christ from the inside out. Religion conforms you to a man–patterned relationship with God. There are thousands of religious denominations from which to choose. Each has it's own pattern for your life. If we choose, however, to be filled with the Holy Spirit, He builds Christ up within us, from the inside out. As He constructs our life into the person of Christ, joy fills our soul. In fact, the Greek word *"chara"* is used here and means "to rejoice." The believer full of Christ will have exultation and exuberant joy. He will be filled with good cheer, mirth, and gladness of heart.

Critical, negative persons will be the opposite. Their confession has set the course of their lives, and they have no real joy. In fact, to be around spiritually joyful people is an affront to them. They do not know how to react without retaliation. How tragic is this existence with no happiness, no true joy. This is why God shows us here how to recognize and pray for people who are critical. He tells us their needs, and He states to us that we must pray for those who are bound by a critical spirit. Oh, the wondrous place in life when ***"the joy of the Lord is my strength."***

Last, but not least, we are to pray for their ***"protection."*** This word brings to mind the involvement of outside forces to hinder any intrusion of privacy or loss of property. This is like police protection. However, in this case, the protection is needed from satanic and demonic intervention into their lives. Words are power. People who speak critical words set into motion forces which bind both the lives of those about whom they are speaking, as well as their own. They also set the course of their own human nature and their own human personality by spoken word.

The devil is always looking for an open mouth. It is primarily through that opening he finds his way into the lives of individuals. Again, it is not what goes into the mouth that defiles, but what comes out. What you say is what you are. ***"For out of the abundance of the heart, the mouth speaketh."*** We must protect ourselves from such persons by prayer and praise. We must also help such persons through prayer and praise.

The most dangerous person in the world to the kingdom of darkness is the individual filled with Christ. His words speak life and power through prayer. Therefore, the devil must fight to change those words into death. So, he works to pull down the person living in Christ's victory by getting him to react in anger. Satan must set up circumstances to make you angry. He has to. Then, when you yield and speak a critical, caustic word or some bitter innuendo, satanic and demonic intervention then comes in through your mouth.

That is why God commands us to pray for people who are critical of other people. Why? Because they need welfare, which means a state of better being. Also, they need happiness, for people who are critical are tragically unhappy and without joy. Thirdly, and most of all, they need protection from being demonized. *K.Y.M.S.* here could be changed to "K.T.D.O." - Keep The Demons Out. To do this, they desperately need Jesus Christ to control their lives.

In continuing to the next part of the verse, God gives us true insight into the person who is negative and what he is really like on the inside. God says that we are to ***"truly pity"*** the individual who is critical. Now, pity is a hard word. I have, over the years, tried to assimilate the full force of that word into this message; to find out its true purpose and meaning. Perhaps the best explanation of the statement is simply that we have sympathetic sorrow for one who is suffering, distressed or unhappy.

In the light of this, here is God's own declaration - we are to pity people who are critical. Why? Because they are unhappy. They are suffering in their souls. God says they are distressed. How tragic to have to live that kind of life - to be, as the Scripture says, ***"... caught with the words of your own mouth..."*** God commands us to pray for and to pity them.

Heaviness

I must share my feelings concerning the pervasive nature of negative confession. In my experience, it has "atmospheric" as well as personal impact. When I get into a place where there has been criticism, or if there is a presence of active negative confession, it becomes almost impossible to stay. There is a cloud of heaviness. This is due to the demonic oppression that feeds on criticism. A person sensitive to demon activity will always know when there is oppression present; and negative confession will bring atmospheric binding by Satan. Words are power! God has shared all through His word that we must not be unkind to each other. We do not have the right to speak a critical word about another person. Again, when you move into a place where gossip or verbal antagonism has been a part of past conversations, you can immediately sense the oppression about you. The Holy Spirit is grieved. The Spirit–filled Christian will notice it immediately.

In the light of this, God shares with us that the "filled" Christian is to pity those who are critical of others. Again, let us qualify the word "pity." It is not a license to bring yourself to a position of feeling you are better than another. Pride is Satan's strongest weapon. On the contrary, it is a test of the character and the quality of your Christian walk. In regard to this, He states that we are to be ***"... truly pitying and loving them."***

In essence, God commands you to love the person who is critical—and that is not only when they are critical of you, but of anyone. He commands you to pray for him. God's Word commands you to stand with that person in prayer, believing that God's Spirit is going to work through his life. You see, the person who criticizes another individual is sick spiritually. Not only that, but, as we saw in chapter 6, critical words can even bring physical maladies upon the life of another person as demonic forces are released into their lives. The tongue speaks only life or death. Therefore, our prayers are simply warfare to bind Satan's conduct in their life. When we speak negatively (death), we give the enemy more ground. When we speak positively (life), we take it away. We must come against it!

Our Inheritance

God continues in ***I Peter 3:9 (Amplified)*** with: ***"For know that to this you have been called, that you may yourselves inherit a blessing (from God)."*** Now, what have you been called to do? God states that we are not only to pity, but to love people who are critical of other people. When someone directs criticism toward you, God expects you to stand in the midst of the conflict and praise God for what he says. You are to thank the Lord for those who thus speak against you. You must ***"never return evil for evil..."*** For you see, by refusing to respond negatively you have the power to defeat Satan. Praise is aggressively attacking the enemy by God's power, and it destroys him ***(Psalm 149:6)***. You are to agree that God's Spirit is moving greatly in the matter and He is doing a work in your heart. As you do so, your walk becomes so supernatural and life–changing that you live in ultimate victory. You are not only victorious but joyful in the encounter.

Again, how you take criticism shows the level of development of your own character. If you are growing spiritually, you will show it in your ability to take criticism. In fact, God says of the experience: ***"You have been called to inherit a blessing and to obtain a blessing as heirs."*** By what? By ***"... never rendering evil for evil, or railing for railing, but contrariwise blessing."*** You see, God's position in your life is for Him to control you completely. The best way to know if He is controlling your life is by that which comes out of your mouth (or does not, for that matter) - ***"For out of the abundance of the heart, the mouth speaketh."*** In fact, as stated before, you are only as spiritually mature as the level of your praise in the midst of your tribulation.

Pay Day

Now, let us look at what God says in the latter part of this verse. He states that we will ***"... obtain a blessing as heirs, bringing welfare and happiness and protection."*** That is our position. That is our promise and, most of all, our calling. We are heirs of God. That means more than just New Testament new birth. It also means we are joint heirs to all that He is, all that He might be, and all that He wants to be through us. We cannot repeat this enough: the evident sign that He is being Himself through us is that we are never critical, caustic or bitter. Our position toward those who attack us and others is to minister to them in prayer warfare, binding the demonic forces that control them.

The biggest problem I face is the desire to run from those who have problems with negative confession. I do not want to hear it. It makes me party to their carnal state. I cannot stand it when someone is critical. I can feel Satan's presence and his effort to bring me down from my walk with Christ.

Again, do not listen to criticism! Pray to bind it when you hear it spoken. Deal directly with the source of the problem. However, love the person who is critical—God commands you to do so. God tells us to minister to these people because they are demonically bound. Many times, I find it difficult to do this. Therefore, if I am to minister to critical people, the Lord must overcoming me and work through me. I bring myself to His presence by praise and adoration. It has to be Him in my life.

The Good Life

Now, let us look at the next three verses ***(I Peter 3:10-12, Amplified)***. Herein are the wonderful rewards of the believer who has control of his confession.

> ***For let him who wants to enjoy life and see good days (good whether apparent or not), keep his tongue free from evil, and his lips from guile (treachery, deceit).***
>
> ***Let him turn away from wickedness and shun it, and let him do right. Let him search for peace—harmony, undisturbedness from fears, agitating passions and moral conflicts—and seek it eagerly. Do not merely desire peaceful relations (with God, with your fellowmen, and with yourself), but pursue, go after them.***
>
> ***For the eyes of the Lord are upon the righteous—those who are upright and in right standing with God—and His ears are attentive to their prayer. But the face of the Lord is against those who practice evil—to oppose them, to frustrate and defeat them.***

The Good Life

The "good life" - What does that phrase mean to you? In the minds of many, it would be a home in the country. To others, retirement with adequate income. Perhaps a place on the ocean, or better physical health.

The good life! The whole world today searches for it. However, they will never find it—except in Christ. We can design, and build, and function, but soon we tire and our excited feelings dissipate into the boredom of "been there, done that." We seek newer horizons and greater adventures in our quest for this dream. However, the good life does not start outside with a new wife or new location. It starts inside. It has its origins in ***Ephesians 2:10***, which teaches us that if we will agree with God for our lives daily and move into His purpose and will for us, we will progress and grow into the good life.

> ***For we are God's [own] handiwork (His workmanship), recreated in Christ Jesus, [born anew] that we may do those good works which God predestined (planned beforehand) for us, (taking paths which He prepared ahead of time) that we should walk in them - living the good life which He prearranged and made ready for us to live (Ephesians 2:10, Amplified).***

The great tragedy of the normal Christian experience of today is that there is, for the most part, a negative relationship to everything. People are critical about each other or themselves. Yet God says in ***I Peter 3:10, "let him who wants to enjoy life and see good days (good whether apparent or not), keep his tongue free from evil, and his lips from guile (treachery, deceit)."***

Herein lies the formula for happiness. It comes to the person who can control and bind himself from speaking negative confessions. If he can overcome his caustic, critical or bitter tongue, he will be the individual who will move into that treasured place so sought after throughout the history of human existence. He will achieve the GOOD LIFE. That existence is not in things exterior, but in a position interior. A better way to say it is that it is not what you own on the outside, but Who owns you on the inside. Victory comes when you learn not to speak until spoken through. At the moment when Jesus Christ, by your choice, has consumed your spoken word, you move into that which is known as the GOOD LIFE—His life. ***"Christ in you the hope of glory," (Colossians 1:27).***

Focus Questions

1. Meditate for a moment on ***I Peter 3:8-12*** in the Amplified Bible. What is the Lord saying to you through this passage? Will it require you to change how you relate to and talk about others?

2. It has been stated that Christians often shoot or bury their wounded. Have you ever felt that Christians rejected and condemned you as you experienced difficulty? Have you ever done that to other Christians? What spirit is at work in this process?

3. What does Satan work to accomplish in the local church? What does God command us to do concerning this matter?

4. Have you ever been in a local church in which serious conflict developed? Did negative confession play a role? How was the situation resolved?

5. In review, what are the only two ways a Christian should speak about others? What is the effect on you when you listen to people

who speak in other ways?

6. How should the Christian react to insults, character assaults, tongue lashings, scolding and beratings if they are deserved? How about those that are undeserved? What gives the Christian the ability to react this way?

7. According to ***I Peter 3:9***, what should we pray for the person who gossips? Why?

8. What sort of forces are set in motion when people speak critical or negative words about themselves or others? What is the effect of these forces on churches, families, and personal relationships in general?

9. What does the Christian have to do to inherit the blessing of ***I Peter 3:9***?

10. What should a spirit–led Christian do when faced with someone who is being critical or negative? Have you ever experienced the unhappy results of not reacting that way?

11. According ***I Peter 3:10-12***, what is the key to the "good life?" What is a five word phrase to describe this condition? Are you experiencing this "good life?"

CHAPTER TEN

Choose Life

Moses was the vessel chosen by God to bring the people of Israel out of bondage in Egypt, and to receive for all mankind the precious, perfect statutes and commandments contained in the Law of God. He was Israel's leader, judge and spiritual guide for forty years. As Moses was about to be taken to the Lord, he recounted and interpreted how the Lord had dealt with His people and challenged the people of Israel to serve the Lord. His final words were.

> ***... I have set before you life and death, blessing and cursing; therefore choose life, that both thou and thy seed may live; That thou mayest love the Lord thy God, and that thou mayest obey His voice, that thou mayest cleave unto Him; for He is thy life, and the length of thy days... (Deuteronomy 30:19-20).***

In this writing, we have laid out what God's Word has to say about positive and negative confession. God is serious about what you say. He has set before you life and death, blessing and cursing. The key to which one you receive is what comes out of your mouth. As we review the teachings of the Scripture covered in this book, I urge you to choose life.

In Review

God commands us to ***"... keep [our] tongues free from evil and [our]***

lips that they speak no guile" (I Peter 3:10). Regarding this, let us look back to a position we discussed in a prior chapter.

In the book of ***Ephesians***, Paul deals with the church in Ephesus about attitudes that lead to godliness. He has shown the depth and width of the power in the believer in ***Ephesians 1***. In chapter 4, he describes the life we are to live to maintain this incredible experience of oneness with Christ. In the light of where we have come to in this writing, let us go over this verse again. You will recall that we dealt basically with ***Ephesians 4:29*** in the area of ***"foul or polluting language."*** Now, from the position of "living the good life," let us look again at ***Ephesians 4:31***. God says:

> ***"Let all bitterness, and indignation and wrath (passion, rage, bad temper) and resentment (anger, animosity) and quarreling (brawling, clamor, contention) and slander (evil speaking, abusive or blasphemous language) be banished from you with all malice (spite, ill will or baseness of any kind)."***

Here he deals almost totally with the confessed word. All of these phrases refer to emotions expressed through confession: ***"bitterness," "indignation," "wrath," "passion," "rage," "bad temper,"*** and ***"resentment" "anger," "animosity," and "quarreling."*** These are outward expressions of an inward experience.

From there, He speaks of ***"brawling, clamor, contention,"*** only to follow with the word ***"slander."*** We get a true picture of how God feels in His use of the word ***"slander"*** by looking at its definition. It means ***"evil speaking, abusive or blasphemous language."*** Evil speaking is negative confession toward another individual by using ***"foul or polluting language."*** Abusive language disturbs or tears down the character of another person. To be abusive is to address someone with words that are insulting and contemptuous. Satan, speaking through a person, uses these utterances to bind them into a negative position.

Then the Lord follows with the phrase ***"... blasphemous language."*** The use of this word is interesting in that it gives a clear picture of how God feels about the human whom He created in His own image. The word ***"blasphemous"*** means by dictionary definition, "involving or marked by debasement or defilement of what is sacred." When we curse man with words, we curse God. To Him, all are sacred. He gave His Son for all. Therein lies the commandment to ***"pray for those who despitefully use you and persecute you."*** Never be negative. Never! ***(Matthew 5:44)***.

Then, of course, we understand that the cursing comes from the inside. People use it as an abusive position, accentuating that position to prove a point. God's commandment is that it be ***"...banished from you."*** The word "banish" means "to completely eradicate, take away, eject by force." Beloved, you are never to be critical of any individual under any circumstance. There is no room for it in the Word of God, or the life of the Spirit-filled child of God.

You say, "Well, you take too much leverage with the Word here." No, I do not. Again, ***"out of the abundance of the heart, the mouth speaketh."*** You can tell who you are and what you are based first on what God says about you, and then, secondly, by what you say about others. The individual who controls his tongue can control his whole body. We have shared that many times in this writing, but you must understand it. God says, literally, these negative things are to be ***"...banished from you..."*** completely. Along with them, ***"... all malice (spite, ill will or baseness of any kind)."*** In this case, all of this deals primarily with the spoken word. You are asking, "What is your point in going over this area again?"

Have you ever heard of the formula for good public speaking? There are two things you must remember here. Number one, Satan can steal the seed (word) sown into the heart, so repetition is the greatest method to insure learning. Second, to saturate an audience with a message, you must tell them what you want to tell them. Tell them and then tell them what you told them. If they are still awake, they will never forget. That is why I keep going over and over these Scriptural positions concerning the power of the spoken word.

What You Speak is What You Live

I ask you again: Do you want to live the GOOD LIFE? You can. How? By *keeping your mouth shut*. By never saying an unkind word, never being critical, never being caustic, never being bitter. Speaking only when spoken through. It all boils down to controlling you tongue; or more accurately, letting Christ control it.

Again, ***I Peter 3:10*** states: "***Let him who wants to enjoy life and see good days (good whether apparent or not)...***" What an incredible statement. The person who will "keep his tongue from evil and his lips from guile (treachery, deceit)" is the one who will experience this promise. If you will notice, God says, ***"Let him."*** It is a positive action on the part of the believer.

To bring it home, you must submit yourself to Christ's (the Holy Spirit's) total control so He can keep your tongue free from evil. What is evil? The volitional participation in something that is harmful, disastrous or anti-God. The father of evil is Satan. For you to be critical is simply to give yourself over to Satan.

Webster states, "Evil is something that brings sorrow, distress or calamity." That is the devastating effect of negative confession. For a person to criticize another person only brings sorrow, distress or calamity.

However, the individual who keeps himself or refrains from speaking negative confessions will enjoy life and see good days. You see, when you speak evil, when you speak criticism, when you speak blasphemous and foul language, it does something to the inner workings of your life and soul. It brings Satan into dominion over your character. Consequently, oppression comes. In that oppression you lose all of your victory and your entire spiritual walk with Christ.

In God's Wisdom and His choice for you, you are to "keep your tongue free." He commands it. To break that commandment is sin and thrusts you into Satan's kingdom of doubt, fear, and hate. Once there, the devil stokes the flames that burn within until they consume you and your life is nothing but ashes.

Deliverance

Going to ***I Peter 3:11 (Amplified)***, God shares with us that we must ***"... turn away from wickedness and shun it ... and do right."*** We must ***"... search for peace - harmony, undisturbedness from fears, agitating passions and moral conflicts - and seek it eagerly..."*** In the light of the prior verses, this could very well have to do with our confession. We are to run from wickedness. We are to run from negative confession. We are to run from speaking negative words. We are to shun it; we are not to have anything to do with it. It is a trap that will destroy us.

A good way to tell your position in Christ is to observe how you handle being around someone who is critical. Do you absorb what they are saying? Is there an interest in your heart to hear the carrion ("dead or putrefying flesh"), or do you find yourself pulling away, crying out in your spirit: "Oh God, get me out of this conversation. Relieve me, release me, deliver me, please." When you are around cursing, does it pierce your heart? Or have you become so compromised and hardened within that it does not bother you anymore? Are you a TV prime-timer without conviction? Oh, how tragic this state of being. It is a backslidden condition away from a spiritual walk. God commands you to turn away from these kinds of things. You are to ***"...cry out for peace and for harmony."*** Does that sound familiar?

God says He wants us to pursue the good life. Only the Christian who can control his confession will live The good life. You live this by keeping your lips from ***"guile,"*** from ***"treachery"*** and ***"deceit."*** The acid test to tell if a person is living the good life is to listen to what he has to say. Listen to his expressed attitude. Listen to his confession. See how he handles hearing negative confession. Does he pray for the other person or does he become bitter about that individual and make negative statements toward him? You can tell where you are in Christ by what emits from your mouth. As I have stated many times and many ways, ***"for out of the abundance of the heart, the mouth speaketh."***

Life or Death—Your Choice

We have tried to share with you that your words are life or death. Men have begun to exploit this today by experimentation into the psychic areas of the personality. Satan is promoting this course in the lives of humans. He knows that once soul power is tapped, men will then begin to experiment in areas that will eventually bring demon possession and satanic dominion over their lives. Thus is the New Age development. This even has infected the church through positive confessions by false spirits of Jesus ***(II Corinthians 11:3-5)***. Words carry life or death. Man manipulating and trying to harness the soulish power of speech will only bring destruction.

When you speak that which is negative about another individual, you set into motion forces that actually bind the lives of people. I know that this is deep doctrine; however, it is a truth Christians need to understand. We can bind other people by speaking negative words about them. This applies for the saved as well as the lost. In fact, it applies more often for the lost who are dominated and have their minds darkened and alienated by Satan ***(II Corinthians 4:3-4)***. We have had many experiences in dealing with those who have broken the spoken word over their lives simply by standing against those words by the Blood of Jesus Christ.

So many times, we have gone into churches where atmospherically in the building there would be a binding force. There was a deep oppression! The reason? Negative confession. This brings the demonic presence of darkness into the atmosphere. However, when we would stand against it by the Blood of Christ, commanding it to leave, we would immediately sense a release in the building. This works. The devil and his demonic spirits are in the atmosphere. He is in the air. In fact, the Bible calls him the prince and power of the air. Negative confession brings demonic presence. Once invited in by criticism, satan and his demons create through wiles an atmosphere of anger and rebellion. Through these killing fields of words he brings his greatest harvest—division ***(Matthew 12:25-27)***.

I have seen people who have bound themselves by spoken word. An example is, "The older I get, the worse I feel." Or, "This is going to be a bad day, and I can feel it or know it." Or, "I know nothing good will come of this." The tragedy of these kinds of statements is that they are instruments used by Satan to bind the life of that individual. They bring bondage to their own lives and then to the circumstances of which they speak. Never be critical, caustic, or bitter! Never speak a negative word about any individual or yourself! Never!

Confession Breaks Oppression and Possession

Learn the process of praise. Begin warfare praying and minister through prayer to another person's life. Do you know of an individual who is without Christ that you want to see born again? Begin to confess the salvation of that individual in agreement with God. Stand in prayer that Satan be bound and can no longer blind the mind of that person ***(II Corinthians 4:3-4)***. Begin to confess that the Spirit of God is breaking the stronghold over their life.

Then I urge you to begin to live for Jesus and make a positive confession for revival about you or your church and the area where you live. You will begin to see things happen. Why? Because you are in agreement with God. You are setting into motion not your soul power, but His "flow" power through your life. Satan will be defeated. Always remember that positive confession will break oppression and demon possession.

Positive or Negative Confession

The spoken word is an incredible power. It can cause great problems through negative confession or great blessing through positive confession. Making negative confessions, particularly words spoken in anger, energizes the soulish power. Angry words are the source or process of the soul's greatest negative force. When the power of evil moves upon you and you make statements in anger, these forces - like missiles - bind others as they are released by the soul. However, by the same process, the individual who walks in the Spirit and has deep love can speak love. Such spiritual love flowing through that person by positive confession will bring life to another person or to a circumstance.

The first evident sign of the Spirit-filled, Christ-controlled and Christ-dominated life is constantly seeking proper knowledge of the Bible. We will study to show ourselves approved. The Bible will become a book (life) with which we fall in love. Second, we will desire to go on with God. We will hunger and thirst for Christ to fill our spirits and operate in our hearts. We will have victory, holiness and perfect love; or better said, Christ's life through us.

Third, we will be fervent in winning souls. Another evident sign Christ has captured your heart is your life's pursuit becomes telling others about Jesus. God says, ***"He that winneth souls is wise."*** Fourth, we need to commit our lives to Christ to such a degree that we see God's flow through us daily. We will walk in the Spirit, be led of the Spirit, and be filled with the Spirit. In the process of that we will begin to minister life. That life will be the resurrection life of faith. In fact, we will live by the Faith of the Son of God ***(Galatians 2:20)***. The level of Christ's control in our lives will be the level of faith's control and ministry through our lives.

Fifth, we are to bind our spoken word to Christ's constant control. We are never to be critical, caustic or bitter or say any unkind thing. We are to walk in the Spirit, but most of all we are to speak in the Spirit. We must never speak unless spoken through. If this fifth evidence of the Spirit-controlled life is not prevalent, the first four are false: ***"For out of the abundance of the heart, the mouth speaketh."***

Those first four things we gave you are widely accepted among Spirit-filled believers. The fifth I have added because I feel it is essential. Again, what you say is what you are. To take the power of the soul and put it in its proper perspective is to daily commit that inner man to Jesus Christ. It is to become a living sacrifice that is ***"... holy, acceptable..."*** We are to coordinate every activity that we have into Jesus.

In doing so, we can then test to see if this is happening by listening to our own words, or the words we listen to. The test is what comes forth from you in standard conversation. The ultimate test is what comes out of you when you are "squeezed" in moments of crisis. Are you critical or do you operate in victory? Is Jesus Christ the Lord of your life? Is Jesus Christ the Lord of your lips? The way to tell this is by what you speak. Learn to bind your words. In every case, in every situation, *K.Y.M.S.* unless Christ is speaking through you.

I trust this writing has brought great conviction to your heart about your own confession. As always when I deal with this subject, it has to mine.

Focus Questions

1. In ***Ephesians 4:31***, God deals with destructive character traits which are outward expressions of inward experiences. What is the primary mechanism that Satan uses to insure that these negative behaviors are expressed? Discuss your experience of the spiritual warfare to rid yourself of these expressions?

2. God commands that these expressions be banished from you. What does this mean? Have you ever experienced the pain that such expressions cause or the joy of being free from them?

3. God says that we are to pursue the Good Life! Do you want to live the good life? How is this done?

4. A good way to tell your position in Christ is to be around someone who is critical. Do you absorb what they are saying? When you are

around cursing, does it bother you? What does God command concerning these kinds of things?

5. List at least four things you have learned that you can do to avoid negative confession. Pray that the Lord will give you victory in these areas and "banish" negative confession from your life.

6. Three key phrases have been repeated often in the book regarding negative confession. What are they?

7. What are the evident signs that we are living a Christ centered life?

8. Your confession reveals your spiritual condition. Are you critical? What comes forth from your mouth in standard conversation or in moments of crisis when you are 'squeezed'? If you are not happy with the answers to these questions, you can be free of negative confession.

Don't bind yourself and others with negative confession. The devil is atmospheric. He and his demons are in the air. Negative confession brings their presence.

Step 1. Confess your sin before God, asking His forgiveness. If your relatives have the problem, pray asking God to break all generational curses of negative confession.

Step 2. If possible, and God gives you permission ask others to forgive you for your negative confession of them. Be careful about this especially if the other person is not aware of what you have said and has not been hurt by it. But in cases where your negative confession has caused strife, division or hurt asking forgiveness is important.

Step 3. Repent. Turn from negative confession by asking God to bind your words. Praise God in every circumstance of your life standing in agreement with ***Romans 8:28 & 29***. Speak of others only in prayer or praise!

Step 4. Pray and study God's Word daily asking God to fill you with His Spirit.

"Does a fountain send forth (simultaneously) from the same opening fresh water and bitter? These things ought not to be so." (James 3:10&11)

Final Note: When you have been set free of negative confession you will find that you can not stand to be around it. When this happens, guard against judging those who are speaking negatively and critically. Love them by praying for them—for their welfare, happiness, and protection. Remember-Words Have Power!

DEATH AND LIFE ARE IN THE POWER OF THE TONGUE!

In Memory of Dr. Mickey Bonner

On June 5, 1997, Mickey Bonner, a much traveled evangelist, died while preaching on the power of prayer and brokenness to Bill Gothard's Advanced Training Institute, held in Knoxville, Tennessee. As he was finishing his sermon, Mickey's last words were, "We must pray with the mind of Christ and it will only come when we humble ourselves before Him. It will only come when we are... broken." With no sign of pain, the Lord instantly took our brother home before 16,000 people. The assistant safety director at the conference said it all with, "He went out in a flame of glory preaching God's word."

Mickey would have had it no other way.

Other Works by Dr. Mickey Bonner

Brokenness, the Forgotten Factor of Prayer—This book reveals God's purpose for humility in the life of the Christian. It will help to open the door to a new and wondrous place in Christ.

Brokenness, the Forgotten Factor of Prayer Study Guide—A companion to Dr. Bonner's book on Brokenness that will challenge you every step of the way as you study this too often overlooked factor to prayer.

Hearing God's Voice from Within—Brother Bonner reveals insightful truths on this subject learned at the feet of the Master during a life committed to prayer. Believers who apply these truths to their lives will deepen their walk with Christ and learn to discern God's voice from within.

Spiritual Warfare Prayer Study Guide—A comprehensive study guide that will teach the Christian how to pray in authority until the answer comes.

Prayer is Warfare—The object of this book is to bring to light one of the most important principles of prayer and that is the conducting of warfare against Satan.

Other Works by Dr. Bonner

The Force that Moves the Hand of God—Just after completing this message, Brother Mickey went to be with the Lord. Many have called this message one of the most powerful that they have ever heard. Dr. Bonner teaches the Christian who they are in Christ. (Available in Video or Audio)

God Can Heal Your Mind—The healing of your mind will come only when you are able to face the dark areas and experiences of you life, and forgive. Learn how to bring every thought into captivity, to the obedience of Christ, ***II Corinthians 10:3-5***.

Video Cassette Tapes, (VHS)—Brother Bonner has video messages on various subjects in the areas of Brokenness, Spiritual Warfare Prayer, God's Power, and the Christian Home.

Cassette Tapes/Compact Discs—Brother Bonner has an extensive library of messages that will deepen your Christian walk.

Ministry Information—For more information about our ministry, our Partners in Vision program, or other materials we have available, please contact us at the:

To Order these materials or for a complete listing of Dr. Mickey Bonner's teaching materials, or for more information contact the:

Mickey Bonner Evangelistic Association

PO Box 680368

Houston, TX 77268-0368

Or Phone: 281-444-7563 Fax: 281-580-0175

Other Materials By Dr. Mickey Bonner
Individual Cassette Messages Or Compact Discs

Dr. Bonner has many messages on the following topics. We have selected just a few of the messages to be listed here. Topics include:

Knowing God's Will for Your Life
Brokenness
Praise and Worship
The Home and Family
Spiritual Warfare and Deliverance
Letting Christ Be Lord
Becoming an Intercessor
Spiritual Gifts
God's Power
Establishing a New Testament Church
The Holy Spirit
Salvation and the Second Coming

Some Selected Titles are:

- ☐ The Meaning of True Brokenness
- ☐ Why We Are to Pray to Be Broken
- ☐ How Brokenness Releases the Inner Man
- ☐ Brokenness—a Gift from God
- ☐ Brokenness—the Road from Death to Life
- ☐ Brokenness—the Beginning of All True Righteousness
- ☐ The Ministry of the Holy Spirit Is Only Through Brokenness
- ☐ Get Off the Streets and Get on Your Knees
- ☐ How to Live by the Power of God
- ☐ The Beginning of All True Ministry
- ☐ Where is Their God?
- ☐ Those Upon Whom God Will Pour His Spirit
- ☐ How We Conquer by Failing
- ☐ Any Old Donkey Will Do
- ☐ How to Test Your Walk with Christ
- ☐ Job—How God Breaks a Man
- ☐ Hidden in the Day of the Lord's Anger
- ☐ How Satan Hinders Prayer in the Christian's Life
- ☐ The Five U's of Unanswered Prayer
- ☐ The Biblical Formula for Prayer Warfare
- ☐ Why You Cannot Hear from God
- ☐ Why You Cannot Hear From God

To Order these materials or for a complete listing of Dr. Mickey Bonner's teaching materials, or for more information contact the:

Mickey Bonner Evangelistic Association

PO Box 680368

Houston, TX 77268-0368

Or Phone: 281-444-7563 Fax: 281-580-0175

What Others Have Said About Mickey's Work...

About Dr. Bonner's Book, *Brokenness, the Forgotten Factor*

"The way to reach God's higest purpose for your life is through Brokenness. Mickey Bonner has captured that message in this book. You will enjoy it!"
John Hagee—Senior Pastor Cornerstone Church, San Antonio, TX

"This book has all the ingredients needed to assist in sparking a National Revival that could spread throughout the four corners of the earth, one person at a time..."
Coach Bill McCartney—Founder/CEO Promise Keepers

"Good work Mickey. *Calvary Road* helped, and this deepens the message."
Dr. Bailey Smith—Former President of the Southern Baptist Convention

"My prayer is that God will use this book to break our hearts and to bless our lives."
Adrian Rogers—Senior Pastor, Bellevue Baptist Church, Memphis, Tennessee

About Dr. Bonner's Book, *Hearing God's Voice from Within*

"In Hearing God's Voice from Within, Dr. Bonner provides the Church with God-given wisdom. Believers everywhere need to learn how to hear His voice! With great biblical insight, Dr. Bonner describes what it means to hear His voice and how to obey Him. I highly reommend this reading."
Dr. Bill Bright—Founder of Campus Crusade for Christ International

Mickey Bonner, through a lifetime of study and prayer was anioted to write this volume.
Adrian Rogers—Senior Pastor, Bellevue Baptist Church, Memphis, Tennessee